T5-ANW-024

Selective Conscientious Objection

Selective
Conscientious Objection

Accommodating Conscience and Security

EDITED BY

Michael F. Noone, Jr.

Westview Press
BOULDER, SAN FRANCISCO, & LONDON

Copyright © 1989 by Westview Press, Inc.

Published in 1989 in the United States of America by Westview Press, Inc., 5500 Central Avenue, Boulder, Colorado 80301, and in the United Kingdom by Westview Press, Inc., 13 Brunswick Centre, London WC1N 1AF, England

Library of Congress Cataloging-in-Publication Data
Selective conscientious objection.
  Includes index.
  1. Selective conscientious objection. I. Noone,
Michael F.
U22.S44   1989   355.2'24   88-201
ISBN 0-8133-7570-3

Printed and bound in the United States of America

 The paper used in this publication meets the requirements of the American National Standard for Permanence of Paper for Printed Library Materials Z39.48-1984.

10   9   8   7   6   5   4   3   2   1

Contents

Acknowledgments   vii

Conscience and Security: An Introduction,
Michael F. Noone, Jr.   1

1   Accommodation to Selective Conscientious Objection:
    How and Why, *Kent Greenawalt*   7

2   The Right to Accommodation: Should It Be
    Legislatively Recognized? *William J. Wagner*   25

3   Selective Service and the Conscientious Objector,
    George Q. Flynn   35

4   A Pacifist's View of Conscientious Objection,
    Gordon C. Zahn   57

5   The U.S. Catholic Bishops and Selective
    Conscientious Objection: History and Logic
    of the Position, *J. Bryan Hehir*   63

6   A Bishop Looks at Selective Conscientious Objection,
    Walter F. Sullivan   81

7   The Good of Selective Conscientious Objection,
    John P. Langan   89

8   Alternative Service: The Significance of the Challenge,
    James L. Lacy   107

9   In-Service Conscientious Objection,
    Edward F. Sherman   117

10 The Moral Judgment, Action, and Credibility
    of Israeli Soldiers Who Refused to Serve
    in Lebanon (1982–1985), *Ruth Linn*   129

Notes on Contributors   153
Index   156

Acknowledgments

The following individuals commented on earlier drafts of this book: Robert Destro, associate professor of law at the Catholic University of America and member of the U.S. Civil Rights Commission; James Finn, editor of *Freedom at Issue* and of *A Conflict of Loyalties: The Case for Selective Conscientious Objection* (1968); Robert E. Rodes, Jr., professor of law at Notre Dame Law School, co-editor of *The American Journal of Jurisprudence,* and author of *Law and Liberation* (1986); James S. Nanney, historian at the U.S. Army Center of Military History; Thomas Alder, President of the Public Law Education Institute and publisher of *The Military Law Reporter* and *The Selective Service Law Reporter;* Thomas R. Folk, major, U.S. Army (reserve), who, as a judge advocate, represented the United States Army in several cases of conscience; Malham M. Wakin, professor and head of the Department of Philosophy and Fine Arts at the U.S. Air Force Academy and author of *War, Morality, and the Military Profession* (Westview Press, 2d ed., 1986); Michael Hovey, Executive Director of the Center on Conscience and War; Brian Johnstone, associate professor of theology at the Catholic University of America; L. William Yolton, Executive Director of the National Interreligious Service Board for Conscientious Objectors, and co-author of *Ministry to Persons in the Armed Forces* (1975); Donald J. Eberly, founder and Executive Director of the National Service Secretariat, and co-editor of *National Service: Social, Economic, and Military Impacts* (1982); and Tim Murphy, colonel, U.S.M.C. (reserve) and President of the Military Law Institute.

We are also grateful to Wallace Sinaiko of the Inter-University Seminar on Armed Forces and Society, who suggested contributors; Charles Maresca and Catherine Noone Hutchison, who participated in the preparation of this book; and to Patricia Wright, who patiently prepared the manuscript for publication.

Michael F. Noone, Jr.

Conscience and Security:
An Introduction

Michael F. Noone, Jr.

Demographic trends indicate that, if the size of our nation's military forces is to be maintained through the 1990s, a larger proportion of the declining number of eligible young men and women must be recruited and retained. Some experts have suggested that it may be necessary to return to conscription in order to achieve the necessary force levels. However, the pool of young people, on whom the military must rely, have had the unprecedented experience of having been exhorted for most of their lives to conscientiously question the use of armed force. Our political and moral systems are in conflict over their right to refuse military service. Ninety-four percent of Americans believe in God and seventy percent attend a church or synagogue.[1] Their religious leaders insist on the individual's obligation to selectively object to the use of military force and urge that the law be changed to protect selective objectors. At present, the legal system recognizes only the conscientious objection claims of complete pacifists, who need not be religiously motivated. Can the conflicting demands of individual conscience and collective security be reconciled?

The American tradition of military service is as old as the colonies themselves, as is the problem posed by the citizen who refuses on moral grounds to participate in that service. In Pennsylvania and the lower counties along the Delaware River, Quaker scruples against the bearing of arms obliged colonial authorities to find an alternative to militia service. By the middle of the seventeenth century, the existence of a buffer zone between Indian territory and colonial population centers discouraged the use of militia, which were essentially village-centered, and encouraged the use of volunteer expeditionary forces who, by definition, did not object to the use of military force. However, New England and Virginia, where the militia system was strongest, remained wedded to the historical ideal of the citizen-soldier throughout the Revolutionary War and its immediate aftermath.

Washington, Hamilton, and those other nationalists who came to be known as Federalists argued for a centralized military force, and the delegates who gathered in Philadelphia in May 1787 to revise the Articles of Confederation resolved to

1

recommend a new constitutional arrangement that included a national military establishment. Although James Madison proposed in 1789, during debates about the Bill of Rights, a clause in the Second Amendment that "no person religiously scrupulous of bearing arms shall be compelled to bear arms in person,"[2] his efforts failed. Since the Constitution envisaged a small national standing army composed of volunteers, supported by a militia regulated by individual states, which could make whatever provisions for pacifist scruples they saw fit, the right of the Federal government to demand military service from those unwilling to give it remained unresolved.

In 1863, a compulsory draft law was adopted by Congress and implemented without challenge in the Federal courts. Those who rioted in opposition to the draft did so, not because their religious sensibilities were offended, but because they refused to risk their lives for what they saw as an alien cause. Members of "peace churches" were exempt by law,[3] as they were in the Selective Service Act of 1917 which exempted from combat duty:

> Those individuals who were found by a local board to be a member of any well-recognized religious sect or organization, organized and existing on May 18, 1917, and whose then existing creed or principles forbid its members to participate in war in any form, and whose religious convictions are against war or participation therein in accordance with the creed or principles of said religious organizations.[4]

Conscientious objection, in order to qualify for legal protection, had thus to be absolute (opposition to war in any form) and religiously motivated—clearly reflecting the same concerns that had motivated the accommodations granted Quakers since colonial days.

The Selective Training and Service Act of 1940 did not require conscientious objectors to be members of a church, but it did require their opposition to war to be based on religious training and belief.[5] In 1948, Congress defined religious training and belief as "an individual's belief in relation to a Supreme Being involving duties superior to those arising from any human relation."[6] However, in the 1965 decision of *United States v. Seeger*,[7] the Supreme Court interpreted the Act to include beliefs which were not based on a belief in God, and in 1970 it ruled in *Welsh v. United States*[8] that deeply held moral or ethical beliefs would warrant a "religious" conscientious objector exemption. The law's exemption provisions were still directed primarily towards the religious beliefs of young draftees. Moreover, the law, like its predecessors since colonial times, was intended to protect only that small group of draft age males who were absolute pacifists. Mainstream religious groups, while subscribing to the belief that some wars or forms of warfare could be contrary to their teaching, had never preached pacifism. However, the debate over the morality of American involvement in Vietnam led a number of mainstream church members to claim exemption from the draft as selective conscientious objectors. In 1971 the Supreme Court refused in *Gillette v. United States*,[9] to interpret the statute to accommodate their claims. There the matter rests today, shorn of its urgency because the United States no longer depends on the draft to meet its manpower needs.

Recently a number of political leaders, recognizing the increased cost of military manpower, and the declining numbers of potential volunteers, have called for a reconsideration of the concept of national service. Any such reconsideration will involve a discussion of the present exemption policy. Should that policy be extended to protect selective conscientious objectors, morally opposed to a particular war or to the utilization of particular weapons? Aaron Wildavsky reminds us that:

> Policy is a process as well as a product. It is used to refer to a process of decision-making and also to the product of that process. Limiting oneself to policy as a product encourages a narrow view of rationality as presentation of results, a view that squeezes a disorderly world into the familiar procrustean formulation of objectives and alternatives. Restricting oneself to process, however, may lead to the opposite evil of denigrating reason, of being unable to account for either the creation of projects or their rationalization as public arguments.[10]

This book draws on a variety of disciplines in order to illuminate the considerations which may affect any change in the present policy—the process as well as the product.

Kent Greenawalt, professor of jurisprudence, in "Accommodation to Selective Conscientious Objection: How and Why" analyzes the potential inductee's claim of selective conscientious objection in order to determine whether it can be legally justified and concludes that it could be. While the policy as a product receives favorable treatment at his hands, he is less sanguine about the process: whether it would be possible to establish a system which could discriminate fairly between honest selective conscientious objectors and those who seek protection for reasons of self interest. He concludes that the Supreme Court's elimination of a "religious test" for conscientious objection was legally appropriate and suggests that self-interested draft avoiders could be discouraged by a system of alternative service sufficiently onerous to discourage all but the morally motivated. His chapter presents a number of problems. Should alternative service be seen as a form of punishment? Is a system of alternative service feasible? Has American society—at least in the eyes of the law—become so secularized that religious motivations are irrelevant? How will individuals make a moral judgment about their participation in military service? How will their religious leaders guide them? Is there any way to judge the veracity of a claim of selective conscientious objection? All these topics are addressed in subsequent chapters.

Professor William J. Wagner, writing on "The Right to Accommodation: Should It Be Legislatively Recognized?" introduces one of the pervasive themes in the book: the 1971 policy statement of the Roman Catholic bishops of the United States on Selective Conscientious Objection. The bishops' statement is important for three reasons: they spoke on behalf of the largest religious group in the United States; they claim the heritage of the just war tradition of Augustine and Aquinas; and their statement is representative of the position taken by many mainstream religious leaders. By comparing the bishops' theological justifications with Greenawalt's analysis of the jurisprudential implications of selective conscientious objection, Wagner illuminates the two different kinds of discourse which may be used to rationalize an exemption for selective objectors.

Greenawalt and Wagner's theoretical considerations are put in a practical perspective in the next two papers. Professor George Q. Flynn, in "Selective Service and the Conscientious Objector," describes the conflicting pressures which affected the process of policy formulation between 1940 and the end of the Vietnam War. Flynn's salutary reminder that the Selective Service System was intended to produce soldiers, not protect conscientious objectors, emphasizes that the moral concerns of the few do not loom large on the horizon of the harried bureaucrat. In contrast, Gordon C. Zahn, a committed pacifist, speaks for those who have been and will be processed by the bureaucratic system. His brief chapter, "A Pacifist's View of Conscientious Objection," describes the effects of the present system on the individuals who have claimed its protection.

Morality, not practicality, is the focus of the next three chapters. J. Bryan Hehir, seen by some as the intellectual responsible for encouraging the Catholic bishops to take a collective public position in support of selective conscientious objection, describes in "The U.S. Catholic Bishops and Selective Conscientious Objection: History and Logic of the Position" how this statement was derived from traditional Catholic teaching, a tradition shared by mainstream Christian faiths and Judaism as well. His concern is not with policy as a product or as a process, but with bringing religion's prophetic vision into the public view and thus to affect the formulation of policy.

In "A Bishop Looks at Selective Conscientious Objection," Walter J. Sullivan, a Roman Catholic bishop, describes his work with conscientious objectors and how his flock refused to respond to his call for application of selective conscientious objection principles to the war in Vietnam. Since Roman Catholics are seen to be more obedient to pastoral guidance than other religious groups, his description of their responses, both during the war and in subsequent surveys of their attitudes towards "peace issues" in 1983 and 1986, is particularly informative since it establishes a persistent and significant gap between the bishops' views and those of the laity. Sullivan attributes this gap to two factors: his flock's recent immigrant status, which causes them to be intensely patriotic; and a failure of education, in that they are incapable of carrying on a moral dialogue with their leaders. Until that gap is closed by time and education Sullivan doubts that religious leaders' calls for moral opposition to particular wars or weapons will have an appreciable effect.

If moral discourse is to be achieved, it will be in ethical terms: of ends and means, and the proper relationship between the citizen and the state, the same vocabulary which will be used in the political arena. John Langan, a professional ethicist, shows how a claim of selective conscientious objection, and the just war rationale on which it is based, create particular analytic problems. In "The Good of Selective Conscientious Objection," he concludes that the abstract policy of exempting selective conscientious objectors is ethically justified; but his analysis, which suggests that the application of the principles in particular cases may lead to indeterminate results (i.e., different persons will, in hard cases, reach contradictory conclusions), raises serious "policy process" problems. Should the legal and political system discourage selfish persons from taking advantage of the SCO exemption in an indeterminate case, even if unselfish conscientious objectors are harmed? That question is also addressed by James L. Lacy, a lawyer and military manpower specialist, in "Alternative Service: The Significance of the Challenge." Lacy is deeply pessimistic: his reading of the Supreme Court's interpretations of the statutes leads him to conclude that the conscientious objection exemption has been made so large as to be unmanageable and that the Vietnam experience with alternative service established that the system could not handle any appreciable numbers of alternative service candidates. If his analysis is accurate, then the most significant problem facing the drafters of a selective conscientious objection provision may be the design of a workable, politically satisfactory system of alternative service. Any system must be acceptable to the public. Their attitude is reflected in the response of one Member of Parliament to protests over the conditions at a conscientious objectors' center in World War I: "We can ill afford in this country to coddle and canoodle around these people."[10]

If the problem of fair treatment of potential inductees is difficult, what of the problem raised by the serviceman or woman who claims conscientious objector status after entering the armed forces? A number of authors allude to the issue; the two final chapters address it directly. Edward F. Sherman, a law professor, discusses "In-Service Conscientious Objection" from the viewpoint of the court system: although litigation during the Vietnam War brought some regularity to the system of processing C.O. applications, he notes both institutional and legal biases which could lead to a lack of respect for claims of conscience. But how are claims of conscience to be respected if one is unable to determine whether they are asserted honestly? In the concluding chapter Ruth Linn, a psychologist, discusses the implications of her work with the Israeli conscientious objectors. Her study was undertaken under near-laboratory conditions since the men she interviewed had previously served in the armed forces and were subject to far more obloquy than their American counterparts in the Vietnam war. Her chapter, "The Moral

Judgment, Action, and Credibility of Israeli Soldiers Who Refused to Serve in Lebanon (1982–1985)," offers the policy-maker a case study in selective conscientious objection which suggests that the process problem of determining credibility remains to be resolved.

The variety of disciplines represented emphasizes the extraordinarily complex nature of the problem which has hitherto been addressed by special interest groups with little or no recognition of the wider issues involved. The authors, in many cases drawing from decades of personal work in the areas of law, defense policy, and ethics, offer a framework for discussing a topic of recurring concern.

Notes

1. "Religion in America", *The Gallup Report,* No. 259, April 1987.
2. 1 Annals of Cong. 749 (J. Gales ed. 1798).
3. Draft Act of 1864, ch. 13, § 17, 13 Stat. 6, 9 repealing Act of March 3, 1863, ch. 75 § 2, 12 Stat. 73, which did not contain a conscientious objector provision.
4. Ch. 15, § 4, 40 Stat. 78.
5. Ch. 720, § 5(2), 54 Stat. 885, 889 (1940).
6. Ch. 625, 62 Stat. 604, 613 (1948).
7. 380 U.S. 163 (1965).
8. 398 U.S. 333 (1970).
9. 401 U.S. 437 (1971).
10. A. Wildavsky, *Speaking Truth to Power: The Art and Craft of Policy Analysis* (Boston: Little, Brown, 1979) p. 387.
11. C.B. Stanton, M.P., 5 HC 86, Col. 835, Oct. 19, 1916.

1

Accommodation to Selective Conscientious Objection: How and Why

Kent Greenawalt

The Basic Issues

Should our legal system provide some way to allow selective conscientious objectors to avoid performing otherwise obligatory acts of military service to which they object? If so, which of the ways to accommodate selective objectors is best? These troublesome questions are the subjects of this chapter.[1] I begin by putting the basic question about accommodation into focus and by outlining the range of possible responses under the law.

Selective Objectors

A "conscientious objector" is someone who objects in conscience to doing what is legally required. The term connotes a sense that one would be committing a grave moral wrong if one performed the required act. Although one's objection in conscience might self-consciously relate to one's own status or characteristics—one might object to fighting against a foreign country in which one's parents still live—the ordinary objection is grounded in a view that what is being demanded is a grave moral wrong more generally. Thus, most pacifists believe that war is morally wrong and most objectors to particular wars believe that the fighting of those wars is morally wrong. Since the central case of a selective conscientious objector is someone who thinks a particular war, or aspect of a particular war, is so gravely wrong that he or she cannot in conscience perform required military duties, I shall concentrate on that case in considering the appropriate legal posture.

A selective objector might be someone whose conscience does not permit any participation in military service; on the other hand, he or she might object only to service in a particular theater of war or operation or to particular means with which combat is being waged.[2] The objection might arise prior to the time one enters military service or when one is already serving. In the latter event, the immediately generating cause might be one's own change of mind about duties one is already performing or has anticipated, or an order to perform duties in situations one did not anticipate when joining the military. Obviously, so long as the draft is not functioning, the practical questions about selective objection concern persons already serving in the military. (A selective objection to a limited war might lead to some selective objection to draft registration, but I shall pass over this complication.)

Alternative Legal Responses

There are three fundamental responses that the law can make to selective conscientious objection. The first, which the law formally now provides, is to treat such objections as irrelevant. One who fails to enter required military service or to perform legally required military duties because he objects in conscience to a particular war, or to tactics used in that war, is guilty of a crime. Whatever accommodations may be worked out in practice, and however often appealing selective objectors may have been treated by sympathetic draft boards as general objectors, selective objection has never been an excuse from conscription or military orders in this country.

We must, however, be careful here. A significant overlap exists between the moral norms of the "just war" tradition, which underlie many instances of selective objection, and the international law of war crimes. Many possible tactics for fighting wars that are widely regarded as immoral are also illegal. An American soldier need not, as far as the law is concerned, obey an order to kill unarmed civilians. He need not obey invalid orders, and an order to commit a war crime is invalid.

The situation is different in respect to claimed justifications for fighting a war at all. As far as I am aware, no one has yet been awarded a defense by a court of his own country based on the theory that an entire war effort the country is carrying on violates international law. Such a claimed defense would meet formidable obstacles in the United States beyond the simple hesitancy of most courts to declare that wars in which their country is engaged are illegal. One obstacle is the rule that as far as domestic law is concerned, Congress has the power to override the internal legal significance of international obligations. Another obstacle is the notion, voiced more than once in response to challenges to the Vietnam War, that the legality of a war is a political question, not appropriate for judicial determination.

In any event, when I say that the law does not treat selective objection as a defense, I mean that when an act of war is legal, or will be presumed to be legal by our courts, one's conscientious opposition to performing that act is not legally relevant.

A second possible legal response to selective objection is to create a special exception from general duties for those who are conscientiously opposed to performing them. This, indeed, has been the long-standing legal treatment of those who are general conscientious objectors to war service. If a person's objection to involvement in war in any form leads to unwillingness to perform combatant duty, he may perform noncombatant duty; if he objects to performing noncombatant duty, he is excused from military service altogether, though he must perform alternative civilian service. The exemption has applied both to those who decline to submit to conscription and to those who seek to leave the military once they are in. The special exemption has involved criteria for application employed initially by draft boards and military officers, and ultimately by federal courts. Whether this exemption should be extended to selective objectors was a subject of intense discussion during the period of the Vietnam War. Congress did not choose to make the extension, and the Supreme Court held that it was not constitutionally required.

One critical question about any exemption of this sort is whether religious belief or association should be among the conditions of eligibility. To oversimplify only slightly, Congress has attempted to limit the exemption for general objectors to persons with some traditional religious belief, but the Supreme Court has interpreted the relevant provision to reach all those with a genuine conscientious objection.[3] Almost certainly, the Court's strong doubts about whether a line between religious and nonreligious objectors would be constitutionally permissible underlay its strained interpretation of what Congress had tried to do.

A third possible response to selective objection is the creation of a self-selecting alternative to the duty to which some people object. What I mean by a self-selecting alternative is an alternative whose availability does not depend on the satisfaction of criteria of eligibility. For example, suppose that anyone subject to being drafted could choose three years of civilian service instead of two years of military service, or that anyone assigned to a particular theater of war would have a right to be sent elsewhere in return for extending his service commitment by an extra year. Alternatives like these could be administered without anyone's judging on whether the applicant was a genuine conscientious objector.

This chapter has two primary messages: first, that some accommodation should be made to selective objectors; and second, that, when feasible, self-selecting alternatives are far preferable to exemptions based on subtle criteria of eligibility.

The Perspective for Evaluation

People have a wide spectrum of views about the appropriateness of modern war as an instrument of foreign policy and about the wisdom of recent and foreseeable uses of military force and threats of force by the United States. Since legislators, and the citizens they represent, will have widely divergent opinions about uses of military force, a systematic attempt to analyze the desirability of exemptions for selective objectors would need to address that question from a number of different perspectives. I shall not attempt that exercise. Rather, I shall mention some attitudes about military force that would be likely to incline one favorably toward granting an exemption. Then I shall concentrate on a different attitude that both raises the issues about selective objection in a sharper form and probably dominates legislative consciousness in most periods of time.

A person who is already convinced that a morally grounded objection to a particular required act is correct is likely to think that an exemption from legal punishment is warranted. This conclusion is not inevitable. A person might think some form of punishment is appropriate when people decline to do what is generally required, or he might suppose that the law is incapable of tracking the line between morally justified refusals to act and morally unjustified refusals to act. But one who thinks a selective objector has made a morally correct choice will not regard the prospect of punishment for the objector with enthusiasm. Generalizing a bit, we can conclude that someone who thinks that a high percentage of future instances of selective objection will be morally correct will probably favor a legal exemption.

We can imagine other persons who will perceive an exemption as indirectly serving objectives that they favor. An outright pacifist may want both to excuse as many young men and women from military service as possible and to introduce legal provisions that will discourage the use of military force. Similarly, someone who believes our present and likely future military posture to be unsound may favor laws that make it harder for the country to fight, and he may support exemptions for selective objectors because he thinks they will have that effect.

No doubt, many of those who most strongly favor selective objector exemptions take one of these views, and their advocacy of exemptions properly includes advocacy of their underlying attitude toward military force. But they cannot expect most members of Congress or highly placed officials in the executive branch to have any of these attitudes. These officials, after all, are the people who decide whether military force will be used and who have the power to stop a use of force that has once begun. Most of them will think that most uses of force by this country are morally and politically justified. They will think that most selective objectors have made a mistaken moral judgment, either in wrongly evaluating the morality of particular military efforts or tactics or in not assigning sufficient weight to the judgments of the community expressed in political decisions, or both. To be successful, an effort to introduce exemptions for selective objectors will have to persuade legislators who think that community judgments count for a great deal and that most of our country's uses of military force are warranted. Many people who think that most selective objectors are wrong in their moral evaluation will need to believe that they nevertheless should be excused, just as many people who think pacifists are wrong now think that pacifists should not be compelled to fight.

This is the perspective from which the rest of this chapter is written. Thus, I do not argue that our present military policy is largely misguided, or that no individual should participate in a war or military operation without a careful judgment that what he or she is being ordered to do is morally justified. Let me repeat that this is not because I think these matters are irrelevant for a full discussion of legal treatment of selective objectors. Rather, it is because I believe it also important to consider what can be said about exemptions to people who believe that selective objectors will not usually have made "correct" moral evaluations, and who may doubt that prospective soldiers, ideally, should exercise as independent a judgment about their country's uses of military force as modern representatives of the just-war tradition urge.[4]

Selective Conscientious Objection and the Reason for Punishment

What reasons are there to exempt selective objectors? At least one way to approach this question is to ask how far the purposes and ordinary minimum requisites for punishment are met when the refusal of selective objectors to comply with legal duties is treated as criminal. In employing this approach, I shall distinguish "refusal to be drafted" from "refusal to perform duties within the military," and I shall comment on relevance of a draft for the duties of those already in the military. I use the present treatment of general objectors as a point of comparison, assuming that a fairly widespread consensus supports their not being subject to punishment if they are willing to perform alternative service. One standard for judging the appropriate treatment of selective objectors is the closeness of their circumstances to those of general objectors. In analyzing the purposes and requisites of punishment, I initially suppose that the class of selective objectors can be identified with complete accuracy. I then address problems of identification.

Moral Blameworthiness

Although it is occasionally asserted that a primary purpose of criminal penalties is to condemn and punish morally blameworthy acts, many acts that are grossly immoral and widely understood to be so are not made criminal. Though a person who accepts this state of affairs might still assert that punishment of immoral behavior remains a positive purpose of punishment, one whose importance happens to be outweighed sometimes by other values, a more defensible position is that moral blameworthiness is a necessary condition of justified punishment, a kind of negative constraint on the legitimate use of criminal penalties to accomplish other purposes. The basic idea is that even if utilitarian purposes would be served by punishment, it should not be imposed on blameless persons. In this respect moral blameworthiness might arise out of the commission of acts that are independently morally wrong or out of the commission of acts that society has authoritatively determined are undesirable.

The selective objector intentionally refuses to perform acts that society has determined are desirable, and his own behavior is based on what most people will probably regard as a mistake in moral evaluation. In one sense, this may seem enough to meet whatever requisite of moral blameworthiness is necessary for criminal punishment. After all, it cannot be that society should excuse everyone who is doing what is morally right in his or her own mind; if that were true, most political terrorists would be beyond punishment. This observation forces us to cast a little more carefully any proposition about moral blameworthiness as it relates to the selective objector's sense that he is doing what is morally required.

The typical selective objector refuses to participate in what he regards as a grave injustice. He acts in a manner that he regards as more consonant with the true welfare of his society than the manner in which he is ordered to act, and his moral values, setting limits on aggressive uses of military force and on excessive tactics, are ones that at some level are widely shared in the community. Such a person is not morally blameworthy in the sense of the typical criminal actor, who consciously places self interest above community interest or fails to constrain himself from doing what he knows is morally wrong. Nor is the selective objector morally blameworthy like most terrorists, in the sense of acting upon value judgments the community rejects as abhorrent. Without supposing that moral blameworthiness in one of these senses is a necessary condition of all justified punishment, we can say that its absence is a strong reason for withholding criminal penalties. It is just this absence that generates the intuitive sense that punishing selective objectors is quite different from punishing those who refuse to perform military duties out of selfishness or personal anger.

From the standpoint of moral blameworthiness, the genuine selective objector is in the same position as the pacifist. Each makes a moral judgment that is rooted in a commonly shared disquiet about military force but that is more rejecting of that force than are most members of the community. From the perspective of moral blame, the reasons for excusing selective objectors are as strong as the reasons for excusing general objectors.

Vengeance

A related point concerns a subsidiary purpose of punishment, satisfying justified anger. Someone who understands the bases for a selective objector's refusal to obey a direction will not be likely to regard anger as an appropriate response.

Others, less understanding, may feel some anger, but the satisfaction of unjustified anger should rarely be a purpose of criminal penalties.

Incapacitation and Reform

An important purpose of much serious criminal punishment is to incapacitate dangerous people who would otherwise commit violations of law. A more controversial purpose is reforming the characters of offenders so that they will be less antisocial. Neither of these objectives makes much sense in relation to the selective objector. If released from the military obligations to which he objects, he poses no danger to the community and his sincere objection to performing military duties hardly evidences a character that in general requires reforming.

Deterrence and Education

A dominant purpose of punishment is the deterrence of illegal acts. Since the firmly convinced conscientious objector believes that suffering very severe consequences is preferable to performing the abhorrent acts that the law requires, the prospect of punishment will usually not work effectively to make objectors perform their legal duties. Some conscientious objectors are susceptible to deterrence, however, because they are not actually willing to act on their convictions and go to jail rather than perform military duties. As to these objectors, deterrence works at a terrible price; their feeling that they have yielded to compulsion and violated deeply held principles is bound to involve serious resentment and loss of self-respect.

In addition to frightening people, serious criminal penalties educate them about what society deems acceptable behavior. Young people growing up in a society that does not exempt selective objectors will be subtly influenced against adopting that position. The same may well be said in respect to general objectors, but the difference between what pacifists and most members of society think is much sharper than the difference between what selective objectors and most members of society think. Many young people may regard a particular war or military tactics as politically unsound and perhaps immoral, but will suppose that their duty as soldiers, or as citizens subject to a draft, is to submit to what the political branches of an overall decent society have demanded of them. The selective objector may differ, first, in taking more seriously his or her responsibility to make a carefully informed moral appraisal and, second, in assigning that appraisal a higher priority for his or her own action than someone who focuses on the authority of political decisions. A systematic refusal to accord any exemptions for selective objectors probably does constitute a considerable constraining influence against people developing their serious moral qualms about military tactics into full-fledged conscientious opposition.

Some obvious points may be made about deterrence and education. If one regards punishing people for the exercise of conscience as highly regrettable at best, it matters a good deal how important any accompanying gains in deterrence and education will be. If selective objectors are excused from military service in the first place, that may cause some inconvenience for the draft, but given foreseeable military needs, any actual undersupply of needed personnel is extremely unlikely. If at some early stage of military training or prior to assignment, soldiers know what wars are being fought and in what ways, and are permitted, depending on the scope of their conscientious objection, to drop out of the military altogether or to avoid objectionable assignments, the direct damage to military operations would probably be slight. Permitting selective objections to be effective on the eve of assignment to a particular military operation or in the midst of actual missions would obviously be more disruptive of military endeavors. An exemption that fully protected the selective conscience would have to operate at any time. Often military operations (for example, the Grenada invasion and the air strike at Libya) are unexpected, and many soldiers may develop selective objections only when they experience how a particular war is carried on first hand. But the direct price of granting an exemption increases as the persons raising it get closer to actual combat.

Deterrence and education need to be regarded from a wider vantage point than the number of people who may be discouraged from becoming selective objectors and the direct effect of that success on military efforts. Broader considerations about conformity are involved, and they cut both ways. A person who thinks that society's having more selective objectors would be bad, were that question to be viewed in isolation, might also believe that the general cast of mind in which selective objection flourishes is a healthy one for a liberal democratic society. Selective objectors take social justice and their own moral responsibilities very seriously. Some might well think a substantial increase of citizens with these attitudes would prove highly valuable in moving toward a better social order, even if one regretted the short term effects of manifestation of those attributes in selective conscientious objection. The successful suppression of selective objection may involve serious costs in terms of conformism and lack of social concern.[5]

On the other hand "conformism" within the military may be viewed as a laudable objective. Soldiers, it is said, are carefully trained to act on orders that they do not question, and general requirements, uniformly enforced, are thought to promote military discipline. The lengths to which such arguments may be taken are strongly suggested by the Air Force's defense of its rule that no personnel must wear headgear inside buildings, as applied to a Jewish doctor's wearing of a yarmulke, a defense that the Supreme Court, surprisingly, found substantial enough to override the doctor's free exercise claim to wear the yarmulke while on duty.[6] If the wearing of yarmulkes is thought threatening to discipline, one can imagine what might be thought about allowing soldiers to opt out of military duties whenever they develop a conscientious opposition to performing them. The independence of mind that such an option would recognize might be seen as strongly opposed to the very cast of mind that military training is designed to implant in ordinary soldiers.

Fairness and Perceived Fairness

Allowing people to escape generally imposed obligations can be unfair to those who must pick up their burdens; a widespread perception of unfairness can be a cause of serious discontent. Are exemptions for conscientious objectors unfair to those who serve? The essential answer to this worry is that genuine conscientious objectors, whether general or selective objectors, are, in an important sense, incapable of bearing the burden of military service to which they object. If it is not unfair for the physically unable to escape that burden, it may not be unfair for those who are disabled by conscience from doing so. But the system is fairer overall if those who are excused are required to bear some roughly equivalent burden that is acceptable to their conscience. This is the main point of alternative civilian service.

The concern with fairness if selective objectors are excused is affected by whether a draft exists. Under a draft, the question of fairness in respect to all those who have been compelled to enter military service is serious, even if it is largely answered by the "disability" of those compelled by conscience and by the provision of alternative civilian service. Absent a draft, the only worry about fairness concerns others who have volunteered for military service, knowing they may be ordered to fight in unexpected situations. Of course, if men are on a dangerous mission, made more dangerous by someone's dropping out, the problem of fairness is acute; a lesser problem arises if selective objections lead people to be assigned to highly desired, undangerous, posts in attractive locales that many others wish to have. But letting volunteers drop from the military altogether at some relatively early stage because they develop conscientious opposition to the country's policies does not create any serious fairness problem if only volunteers serve.

Closely linked to actual unfairness is the problem of perceived unfairness. It is undesirable if people who bear onerous burdens believe others are unfairly escaping those burdens. Again, this problem is most significant when a draft is in place; but those voluntarily in military service may feel demoralized if they see others dropping out when some highly dangerous or unpleasant mission is on the horizon.

Generally speaking, the problem of perceived unfairness is likely to be somewhat greater in respect to selective objectors than general objectors. The reason is that a pretty sharp gulf separates pacifists from those who accept the country's use of military force. Much less separates selective objectors from others who have moral qualms about a war effort or particular tactics. These latter may feel that what mainly distinguishes them from selective objectors is a willingness to accede to community judgments, and they may have a greater sense of unfairness if selective objectors are accorded some kind of privileged treatment than if general objectors are. This is part of the slight truth that lies underneath the confusing and mistaken claim that selective objection is political rather than religious.

Problems of Identification

Problems of deterrence, unfairness and perceived unfairness loom larger once difficulties of identification are introduced. One reason not to excuse genuine selective objectors is that some people falsely claiming to be selective objectors will also be excused. And whatever is the reality, if others believe false claims are being sustained, their sense of unfairness will be considerable. Identification of selective objectors may reasonably be thought substantially more difficult than identification of general objectors. One must not only decide whether someone is telling the truth about aspects of the military effort that he finds morally objectionable; one must also decide whether these objections underlie a genuine and overwhelming claim of conscience not to participate. If a soldier has self-interested reasons, including fear and likely deprivation, to avoid particular military duty, it may be impossible or highly difficulty for him to decide if he is also conscientiously opposed to serving as well.[7] For an outsider to try to make that judgment can be a daunting task.

Summary

We have seen that certain reasons for punishment can be served by holding selective objectors to generally imposed military duties, and that the strength of those reasons varies depending both on whether a draft exists and on the point at which the objector seeks to be excused from military duty. We have also seen that strong reasons exist for excusing selective objectors, reasons that closely resemble in both content and strength the reasons already accepted as decisive for general objectors. If serious fairness problems can be met by imposing alternative burdens, these reasons warrant some accommodation to selective objectors.

Techniques for Avoiding the Clash
of Duty and Conscience

Exemptions Given to Those Who Meet Stated Criteria

The traditional approach to conscientious objection has been to exempt persons who fall within a certain classification. While alternative noncombatant service and civilian service have been employed to lift the sting of unfairness, administrative and judicial determinations of whether applicants fall within the eligible class have been critical aspects of the system.

There are three related objections to virtually all such schemes. First, the lines of exclusion and inclusion tend to be hard to defend, especially at the edges of coverage. Second, any system of human determinations involves occasions of misidentification. Third, those who do the administering may be biased in favor of some sorts of applicants and against others.

I shall now briefly survey the issues of classification involving selective objectors. This survey serves the dual purpose of aiding thought about what a desirable classificatory scheme would be, if one were used, and of illustrating the pitfalls of any approach of this kind. I shall assume that a determination has already been made that an exemption both from the draft and from continuing military service of various sorts should be extended beyond general objectors, and that the critical questions are how to classify the eligible selective objectors and outline the ambit of their exemptions. I shall not address here the provision of alternative civilian service, assuming that such service is not a critical part of an exemption absent a draft but would be very important were the draft reinstituted.

Conscientiousness and Sincerity: I assume that one could not qualify unless one were genuinely and conscientiously opposed to serving. First, there is a question of straightforward sincerity. Is the applicant telling the truth or lying about his beliefs? At one time, draft boards and military officers were relatively free to disbelieve applicants but by the end of the Vietnam War, some objective basis in the record, usually not easy to find, was needed before a rejection on grounds of insincerity would be upheld.

The question of conscientiousness is a related but distinct question. One may be honestly opposed to a particular war or particular military tactics and believe it would be morally better not to participate, without having an objection that rises to a conscientious one. Though it is hard to say exactly what it takes to make a conscientious objection, one must at least believe that one should suffer a very serious harm to oneself rather than perform the act in question. This notion is graphically represented in the typical pacifist's belief that he should die rather than kill someone else in war. If very serious penalties loom as the likely response to failure to perform a duty, the person considering refusal has a powerful test of the degree of his moral objection, though some genuine objectors may lack the strength of will to accept the penalties they think they should accept rather than performing the act in question. When, instead, an exemption is available, a person will find it harder to sort out whether his beliefs are intense enough to amount to a conscientious objection. That inquiry may also be very difficult for a fact-finder who assumes that an applicant's report of his general moral beliefs is accurate.

Any test that exempted all people who object on moral grounds to particular wars or tactics would be too broad, virtually making political disagreement a basis for avoiding military service. Therefore, with a qualification discussed in the next section, the present requirement of conscientious opposition appropriately would remain; but how that requirement applies in practice to selective objectors is somewhat more troublesome than the analogous application to pacifists.

Grounds for Conscientious Opposition: Difficult questions arise over which selective objectors should qualify. Should one have to believe that what the government has actually done is seriously immoral or would other bases for exemption apply? I shall briefly discuss three sorts of problems here.

The first concerns "personal" grounds for being opposed to serving. Suppose one cannot conscientiously fight against a country in which one's relatives live. A person with this belief may be as opposed to serving as someone who thinks a particular war is immoral, but it seems doubtful than an exemption should be extended to everyone who feels emotionally that they cannot fight in a particular situation. Probably an exemption should be limited to persons who think a war or particular tactics are wrongful.

The second sort of problem concerns simple factual mistakes. Some pacifist views reflect deep factual disagreements with nonpacifists, such as whether the unitary renunciation of war by a powerful country like the United States would, over the long run, be conducive to human liberty and happiness. But neither pacifists nor nonpacifists can plausibly claim that their opponents are demonstrably incorrect. Selective conscientious objection, on the other hand, could be grounded in some clear mistake of fact. Suppose an objector who did not quibble over definitions of military targets believed wrongly that bombing was being directed at nonmilitary targets. At a minimum, an applicant with factual grounds for his selective opposition should have no right to succeed until he considers evidence presented by the military that is contrary to his factual supposition. Should he receive an exemption if he sincerely clings to a view of the facts that a reviewing officer or tribunal concludes is clearly erroneous? Probably the answer is "yes." The aim of the exemption is to accommodate genuine claims of conscience. Even a stubbornly misinformed conscience should be accommodated. Further, allowing claims to be rejected if based on clear mistakes in fact introduces the disturbing possibility that military officers and review boards will find the facts to be clear when in reality they are far from clear.

The third problem concerns belief that what one is asked to do is illegal. This problem involves both the appropriate grounds for conscientious claimants, and a question whether an exemption should extend to a limited group beyond conscientious claimants. According to ordinary principles in our legal system, ignorance of the law is no excuse. One who disobeys an order on the grounds that it is illegal has a defense if the order turns out to be illegal, but is without an excuse if the order is proper. We can imagine someone refusing to participate in a particular military action that he judges to be illegal. How should this reason for refusing to act compare with a conscientious objection on moral grounds?

In some cases, the belief in illegality will complement or underlie a conscientious opposition. Since moral concepts of just war overlap substantially with the law of war, a person's claim that actions are illegal may coalesce with his conscientious objection on moral grounds. In that event, the objector's legal opinion will be superfluous if the moral objection is sufficient to be excused. In other situations a belief in illegality may constitute the grounds for conscientious objection. A soldier might say: "I would be willing to perform these acts if they were not illegal, but given the judgment of the international community, reflected in the law of war, that they are wrongful, my conscience forbids me to perform them." Such an objection lies very close to the more straightforward claim that the facts are simply so immoral they should not be performed. Thus, a conscientious objection grounded in belief that acts are immoral because they have been made illegal should qualify for an exemption; and, for reasons given in connection with factual mistakes, this conclusion should hold even if the legal judgment is obviously erroneous.

When a person refuses to perform acts because of their claimed illegality but does not assert that his conscience forbids him to do the acts, the right approach is more troublesome. One might say that the person simply must perform the acts or take the risk of being wrong on the legal question, since he is not really a conscientious objector and a mistake about the law would not yield a defense. But this seems to be cutting matters very fine. It may make more sense to say that if a person who is conscientiously opposed to performing military acts is to be excused, a person at the same stage who has a firm and considered judgment that the acts are illegal should also be excused.

The Relation Between the Conscientious Opposition and the Scope of An Excuse: As a matter of principle, the exemption given to a selective objector need go no further than the range of his objection. Some people who object to a war the country is fighting may be unwilling to serve at that time anywhere in the military, but others may be willing to participate in other parts of the world. The scope of an exemption should ideally be tailored to the scope of the objection. It is, of course, possible that administrative considerations will dictate otherwise. Suppose a person strongly objects to any efforts that will directly support the use of napalm. If napalm is being used in a theater of war, higher officials may not want that soldier in that area even if there is a good chance he will never have to directly support napalm use. More generally, the services might make the judgment that it is better not to have as soldiers persons who have developed firm convictions against particular wars or the deployment of particular weapons.

The Stage of Assertion: Probably the most important and difficult question about selective objection is at which stages a person should be able to assert it. Unfortunately, this question is also the one about which someone unfamiliar with military life can say the least that is useful. I assume that when someone is on a dangerous patrol, he should not be able to refuse his sergeant's orders on the grounds of conscientious objection. Even though such an objection might arise at any time, and indeed might realistically be triggered by horrifying experiences in combat, a claim to a legal exemption would have to arise and be made at some remove from active combat. Of course, anyone sympathetic with the principle of selective objection will want to have the objection considered at the latest stages feasible, refusing to yield to every claim about military discipline and convenience, but some reasonable accommodation to military necessity must still be struck.

Should There Be a Religious Basis for the Claim? The question whether a selective opposition should have to be religiously grounded must be considered in light of the evolution of the exemption for pacifists. Earlier in our history, conscientious objectors had to be members of pacifist denominations to qualify for an exemption. Congress then required a religious basis for objection to participation in war, defined in 1948 as a belief in relation to a Supreme Being.[8] In two giant steps the Supreme Court first said that a belief could qualify under the statute if it occupied a place in the life of the believer similar to that a Supreme Being occupies for someone who believes in a Supreme Being, and then said that virtually any person conscientiously opposed to participation in war counts as religious.[9] These extraordinary exercises in statutory interpretation were commonly assumed to reflect strong constitutional doubts both about a line between believers in a Supreme Being and other religious objectors and about a line between religious and nonreligious objectors. In the second case, three justices said that Congress had definitely intended to draw the latter line and that such a line was constitutionally acceptable, because it flowed from a permissible accommodation to religion. In any event, the present statute, shorn of the Supreme Being clause by Congress, still contains an ostensible religious qualification but one that has been vitiated by judicial interpretation.

This legal posture presents considerable barriers to trying to limit selective objection to persons whose objection is religiously derived in some traditional sense. It would be unwieldy to have exemptions for general objectors not depend on religious bases while exemptions for selective objectors required such bases; and attempting to alter the present law for general objectors would be both somewhat complicated (how does Congress say it really means "religious"?) and of uncertain constitutionality.

It has been argued in favor of a selective objection limited to religious believers that those with traditional religious views are likely to have more intense conscientious objections and that a limitation of this sort will prevent the exemption from becoming too political and too unpalatable. But deciding exactly who qualifies under a traditional notion of religion would be exceedingly difficult and the moral evaluations that underlie many judgments of religious believers about "just war" are closely similar to the moral evaluations some nonbelievers may make. For these reasons, because the argument about comparative intensity of feeling of believers and nonbelievers seems unpersuasive, and because trying to undo the effect of prior interpretations of the statute would be cumbersome, I am strongly of the view that any exemption for selective objectors should have no "religious" requirement beyond that presently used for general objectors.[10]

Self-Selecting Exemptions

These various difficulties in defining the scope of an exemption constitute powerful reasons to look for some alternative approach, as do the inevitable difficulties of administering any standard that is legislated. Misapplications are bound to occur, applicants and others will have grounds to doubt whether treatment under the standards is fair, and some who perform stated duties will feel that successful applicants have unfairly escaped them. A self-selecting alternative can avoid all these difficulties. The point is easiest to make with respect to the draft. Suppose any draft registrant can choose between a certainty of two years of civilian service against a chance of two years of military service, or that someone whose number has already been picked can choose three years of civilian service or two years of military service. The choice must be structured in a way that while anyone is free to choose not to do military service, few persons without strong objections will make that choice.

In that event, none of the thorny dilemmas about proper categorizations need be faced; dangers of misidentification will not arise. No one can feel he is treated unfairly because the choice not to serve is available for all, including him. I shall not here try to defend at length the fairness of this scheme for the objectors themselves, and its constitutionality. The gist of defense is that less favorable conditions for those who choose against military service is a proper technique for accommodating those who powerfully oppose serving—much less harsh than a jail sentence—and is the only feasible method of avoiding the unwholesome aspects of legislative categorization and uneven administration determinations.

Once someone is in the military, the alternative for avoiding prescribed service might be an extended term, or lower pay and benefits, for other military duty or some alternative civilian duty. Again the principle would be to make the choice available to everyone, but to set conditions so that few other objectors would be inclined to choose against ordinarily prescribed military duty.

I certainly do not want to claim that any such scheme would work for all stages of military duty; the dangerous mission remains an intractable problem. But it is at least possible that some self-selecting alternative could work at any stage at which an exemption based on categorization would also work.

This essay is not the place to work out details. But a society that prides itself on autonomy of choice and fears government determinations concerning the inner recesses of the minds of citizens should welcome an avenue that is sensitive to claims of conscience without undertaking difficult categorizations and uncertain administration determinations. Accommodation should be made to selective objectors, but, so far as possible, that accommodation should take the form of alternatives available to all, rather than the expansion of a system of categorization and administrative determination.

Notes

1. This essay is not intended as a research paper. Thus, I have been very sparing with citations. Most of the views I express here are developed at greater length in K. Greenawalt, *Conflicts of Law and Morality* (N.Y.: Oxford University Press, 1987), pp. 311–330; Greenawalt, "Conscientious Objection and the Liberal State," in J. Wood, Jr., ed., *Religion and the State* (Waco, Texas: Baylor University Press, 1985), pp. 247–267; Greenawalt, "All or Nothing At All: The Defeat of Selective Conscientious Objection," in P. Kurland, ed., *1971 Supreme Court Review*, pp. 31–94. The last piece treats the statutory law and cases in some detail; there has been little important change in the law governing conscientious objection in the interim. An excellent short piece exploring the arguments about exemption for selective conscientious objectors is James F. Childress, "Conscientious Objection to Military Service," in R. Fullinwider, ed., *Conscripts and Volunteers* (Totowa, New Jersey: Rowman and Allanheld, 1983).

2. An objection to particular means of waging war might lead one to object to service in certain units even when the country is not at war. Someone who objects in conscience to any use of nuclear weapons might be conscientiously opposed to service with strategic nuclear forces.

3. The 1940 Selective Service Act, 54 Stat. 889, exempted anyone "who, by reason of religious training and belief, is conscientiously opposed to participation in war in any form." In 1948 Congress amended the statute to provide: "Religious training and belief in this connection means an individual's belief in relation to a Supreme Being involving duties superior to those arising from any human relation, but do not include essentially political, sociological, or philosophical views or a purely personal moral code." Section 6(j) of the Selective Service Act of 1948, 62 Stat. 613. In *United States v. Seeger*, 380 U.S. 163, 176 (1965), the Supreme Court held that a belief qualifies if it "occupies in the life of its possessor a place parallel to that filled by the God of those admittedly qualifying for the exemption." In *Welsh v. United States*, 398 U.S. 333, 343–44 (1970), decided after Congress had eliminated the Supreme Being language that the *Seeger* Court had rendered ineffective, a plurality of the Court held that purely ethical or moral beliefs could qualify if they impose "a duty of conscience." Justice Harlan concurred on the ground that Congress' attempt to treat religious and nonreligious beliefs differently was unconstitutional. 398 U.S. at 358.

4. Among the Roman Catholic documents eloquently presenting the moral responsibility to exercise such judgment are the National Conference of Catholic Bishops' *The Challenge of Peace: God's Promise and Our Response*, pp. 6–7, 26–37 (1983); United States Catholic Conference, *Human Life in Our Day*, pp. 42–44 (1968); United States Catholic Conference, "Declaration on Conscientious Objection and Selective Conscientious Objection" (1971).

5. *Human Life in Our Day*, note 4 supra, at 43, talks of being "reassured by this evidence of individual responsibility and the decline of uncritical conformism."

6. *Goldman v. Weinberger*, 106 S. Ct. 1310 (1986).

7. This problem is discussed in Childress, note 1 supra, at 160–62; and in Dr. Linn's chapter in this book.

8. See note 3.

9. See id.

10. My own views on the constitutional definition of religion are developed at some length in Greenawalt, "Religion as a Concept in Constitutional Law," *California Law Review* (September 1984), 72:753–816.

2

The Right to Accommodation:
Should It Be Legislatively Recognized?

William J. Wagner

In their "Declaration on Conscientious Objection and Selective Conscientious Objection" of October 21, 1971,[1] the Catholic bishops of the United States acknowledged that their proposal of accommodation for selective conscientious objectors required translation from moral into appropriately jurisprudential terms before it could be enacted as law. In the bishops' words, a prerequisite to enactment is "a policy which can reconcile the demands of the moral and civic order concerning this issue." Professor Greenawalt's chapter, "Accommodation to Selective Conscientious Objection: How and Why," makes a significant contribution to rephrasing the problem in the required jurisprudential terms.

Defining the Perspective Necessary for the Evaluation of Justifiability of the Exemption

Professor Greenawalt's chapter contributes in a number of different ways to the resolution of the jurisprudential challenge acknowledged by the bishops in their statement, but makes one contribution in particular that is fundamental: he specifies the *perspective* appropriate for evaluating the justifiability of the proposed exemption. While the bishops have acknowledged that the appropriate perspective is other than what they alone can offer, their documents have not shown particular insight into the nature of the perspective necessary. In fact, the two alternative perspectives for evaluation of the proposed exemption sketched by Greenawalt and, I believe rightly, set aside by him, are much in evidence in the bishops' documents, particularly in their pastoral letter, *The Challenge of Peace: God's Promise and Our Response.*[2]

The bishops on the one hand adopt the perspective of the moral theologian who begins with the moral principles relative to the individual conscience and extends outwards to evaluate the morality of political action. In this regard, the bishops tend to think in terms of what Greenawalt calls "the paradigm of the morally grounded individual objection that is correct." On the other hand, influenced by the theology of nonviolent resistance of Mahatma Gandhi, they also appear to treat selective conscientious objection as one of a variety of tools available to effect a change in policy. In this respect, they tend to think in terms of what Greenawalt calls the "indirect service" of other goals.

These perspectives have validity perhaps in other contexts, but when introduced in conjunction with legislative proposals, they are destructive and will never result in the enactment of the SCO exemption. Greenawalt correctly suggests that the appropriate perspective for the evaluation of the exemption is rather the framework proper to those responsible for making law. Such a perspective is distinguishable from the framework within which the individual objector comes to his or her personal moral decision, and obviously is not one which can accommodate attempts at subversion through nonviolent resistance.

Professor Greenawalt presents the adoption of this perspective as a tactical necessity, inviting the advocates of SCO to see that individual legislators will operate on the assumption that their decision to wage war is justified and that the moral judgment of the objector is mistaken. Tactically speaking, no argument can succeed if it is not convincing to legislators who assume a mistaken moral evaluation by the individual selective objector. There is no question that this is good tactical advice.

I would like to suggest, however, that there is a deeper theoretical justification for the perspective for evaluation that Greenawalt suggests as necessary, and that this theoretical justification can be developed in a way that both further enhances the general jurisprudential evaluation of the SCO proposal and also assists in assessing the strength of Professor Greenawalt's particular proposed rationale for accommodating the exemption.

The Theoretical Justification of Greenawalt's Proposed Evaluative Perspective

Tactically speaking, the advocate of the exemption must anticipate a clash of personal opinion with the legislator. But this is not all that distinguishes the perspective of the legislator from that of the objector. The lawmaker is responsible for evaluating the justice or morality of the law in a comprehensive way. The objector does not share this responsibility, and indeed is not authorized to exercise it. The objector has, of course, a political right and duty to vote based on what he or she believes justice requires of law. But, the only moral decision he exercises is his personal moral decision to participate or not to participate in a war effort.

The legislator, by contrast, must, as the authorized representative of the community, decide what law to enact as moral or just. The criteria he or she refers to in making this decision are proper to the evaluation of the justice of law and distinct from those governing the justice or morality of individual action. I propose to articulate, in a provisional way, the criteria of a just law to which the legislator ought to refer as relevant to the question of exemption for selective conscientious objectors. While I would ground these criteria in a natural law mode of moral reasoning, either these or similar criteria could be affirmed within a variety of different systematic approaches to the moral justification of law.

There are four such criteria relevant to the present problem. These are as follows:

1. The effect of a law ought to support the preservation of the rule of law within the society. This requirement is concerned with the maintenance of an attitude of respect for the obligatory character of law in the citizenry, but also with endowing the authorities with the means effectively to bring coercion to bear in enforcing the law where appropriate and necessary.
2. The effect of a law ought to sustain the rule of law in society against external aggression. Thus, the common defense is a fundamental moral imperative of lawmakers on the national level at least.
3. The effect of the law ought to be the restraint of the law's coercive force in accordance with respect for the rights and personal moral dignity of citizens, and other relevant moral norms (such as the just-war theory). As just-war theory is relevant to the legislators' assessment of the morality of a proposed military action, the separate principle that coercive power ought to be exercised under the constraint of respect for the rights of citizens is relevant to a decision to grant a SCO exemption.
4. Law ought to be made in such a way that burdens imposed by law are allocated among citizens in accordance with the norm of distributive justice.

An assessment of the justice of a proposed SCO exemption should begin *not* with the just war theory, but with some such set of principles as I have articulated just now. Such criteria can only be applied by a prudential calculation involving the balancing of the demands of these partially competing criteria.

The Justification of the Selective
Conscientious Objection Exemption

Greenawalt's evaluation of roughly these criteria does not permit him to justify an SCO exemption in a strong sense, primarily because of the impact of such an exemption on the principle that laws should be made in such a way as to preserve respect for the rule of law (as implicated in the imposition of general obligations). Instead, he suggests a weak form of justification that amounts to excuse or dispensation from penal consequences of noncompliance with the military service obligation.

Professor Greenawalt's subtle analysis of "the grounds for punishment question" is cogent with respect to the related question of appropriate treatment of certain benign forms of civil disobedience. Cogency with respect to this related question is highly relevant, since the Catholic bishops envision civil disobedience as a matter of personal conscience even where no exemption is recognized by law. No matter how generous the exemptions that are provided, some conscientious dissent will spill beyond what the exemption is able to accommodate. How this civil disobedience is treated under the law is important.

With regard to justification of a SCO exemption, however, I do not find the argument convincing. If the exemption is formally provided for, the individual is freed of the status of law breaker. Professor Greenawalt's analysis may justify only nominal penalties for law breaking, but it does not justify the further step of sparing the individual the status of transgressor. On the other hand, if one promulgates "exemption" merely as a prospective dispensation from punishment (and I do not see how this would really be feasible), then the SCO remains under a cloud of opprobrium. I do not see this as appropriate.

I believe that the exemption can and should be justified in a strong sense. Such a justification could be based in the norm that the law ought to be made in a way that respects as far as possible the *moral integrity of citizens*. I see this as quite a different value than that of "autonomy of choice and protection from governmental intrusion in the mind of the individual" cited by Professor Greenawalt at the close of his chapter.

This norm has long been given important recognition in our tradition. It is recognized as an aspect of the free exercise of religion and is given a degree of protection under the First Amendment. I describe this aspect of free exercise as the right to preserve one's individual moral integrity. Where compelling state interests justify subordinating the right, the legislature still recognizes that the value should be permitted where prudentially feasible. Thus, the value is recognized in the traditional exemption given to general objectors. The exemption has a long history and goes back to the recollection of the mistreatment of left-wing Reformation groups by the European powers, as a paradigm of tyranny. When the value is recognized either as constitutionally mandated, or as legislatively approved, what is being protected is not the freedom of individual choice, but rather the individual's moral integrity in trying to do the "right thing" according to conscience.

The same value is at stake in the proposal of accommodation for selective objectors. Yet, because of a bias deep in American consciousness, this is difficult for many to understand. First Amendment protection of conscience extends the farthest where the claim appears to be an utterly nonrational intrusion of a sectarian claim. For the claim to be recognized in the selective objector context, clarification and persuasion are, therefore, required.

The claim to be protected is *not* the individual citizen's divergent assessment of the morality of the state's action. It certainly is not the right to interfere or defeat the duly chosen policy of the legislature by nonviolent resistance. Rather, the claim to be protected is that of the individual not to be coerced personally to participate in an action he or she believes would be morally wrong for him. Professor Greenawalt recognizes this value in the course of his discussion of the costs of punishing conscientious objectors to deter future individual refusals of general obligations.

The imperatives that the rule of law be respected and the common defense be secured impose definite limits on the extent of the accommodation that can be given individual conscience. Thus, the First Amendment right protected in *Wisconsin v. Yoder*,[3] is subordinated to state interest in *Gillette v. United States*,[4] and *United States v. Lee*,[5] where the government's power to raise taxes and wage war were implicated. In the past, these limits have been thought, as a matter of legislative prudence, to permit general but not selective objection. This is because of the bias mentioned above in favor of a nonrational, sectarian definition of conscience, but also because of the greater threat seen in selective objection to the rule of law, the common defense, and distributive justice. As Professor Greenawalt shows, SCO does generate special grounds of concern in each area.

Properly understood, SCO need not threaten respect for the rule of law. In fact, SCO, while aimed toward vindicating the law's respect for individual conscience, has a strong cross-validating effect with respect to the rule of law. There are two grounds for this cross-validating effect: (1) fidelity to conscience affirms the capacity of individuals to acknowledge the morally obligatory character of the law, in the nonexceptional case; and (2) fidelity to moral analysis of the conduct of war is intrinsically related to the norms of international law, as Professor Greenawalt points out.

This implicit reference to international law validates the rule of law within the national framework by implication. The Catholic bishops stress the dynamism of the world order to a state of international law in connection with every public statement they have made favoring conscientious objection. In this respect, the Catholic proposal is clearly different from the pre-existing Peace Church support of general objection. Individual conscience is not the only value at stake, but the value of responsiveness to higher secular legal norms is also very much at issue.

As Professor Greenawalt notes, there is no realistic chance for an individual American to defend noncooperation in American courts by reference to international law. The freedom of the individual soldier to plead invalidity as a justification of disobedience is, practically speaking, of very minor value relative to the scope of conscientious objection which may arise, and which may in fact retrospectively be shown to have ample support under international law.

By granting the SCO option, the government would be provided the only plausible avenue of practical recourse for the soldier objecting to policies as against international law. (By providing the exemption, the government would be affirming the Nuremberg principles.) When the individual took advantage of such an exemption, he would, therefore, indirectly be validating the rule of law.

Still, the exemption is not yet justified by these cross-validating characteristics alone. If the exemption was *perceived* as allowing certain citizens to ignore the rule of law in principle for self-interested reasons, this alone would warrant a refusal of the exemption. However, by taking symbolic considerations into account in choosing a form of accommodation, one could adequately prevent such a perception. I agree with Professor Greenawalt that one cannot decide whether the recognition of SCO is justified in the abstract, but can only decide the justifiability of concrete forms of accommodation.

The bishops, for their part, would much strengthen their case by expanding their focus to include a stress on the presumptive legitimacy of democratic decisions about the morality of war. Such a presumption in favor of the moral decisions of political authority in this area has traditionally been a part of Catholic just war doctrine. Perhaps the single most radical innovation in the bishops' pastoral letter, *The Challenge of Peace*, was the deletion of this presumption. They nowhere include this presumption among the elaborate set of presumptions they propose in the pastoral to guide individuals in decisions of conscience. In addition, they would strengthen their case if they were more careful to separate a latent interest in the potential of nonviolent resistance as a method for influencing policy from legislative proposals for SCO.

It is interesting to note that in their recent pastoral on the economy[6] the bishops stressed the need for something of a maximalist state. But, by not stressing this principle of the presumptive validity of democratic decisions they remove the necessary foundation for such extensive political cooperation and state action. To some extent, the bishops are displaying the human desire to have it both ways.

The threat to the principle of the rule of law is, however, only one objection to the recognition of SCO. A second objection relates to the criterion of distributive justice, as Professor Greenawalt demonstrates. It is an inescapable fact that the selective objector incidentally receives relief from a significant burden, namely increased hardship and numerous injuries, including death. The unfolding saga of the after effects of combat in Vietnam shows the great costs that these veterans are even now paying and that selective objectors would have avoided. An exemption can be justified, only if the form of accommodation substitutes burdens for those incidentally evaded by the SCO. Here I agree closely with Professor Greenawalt's analysis. The threat of SCO is on this count probably greater than that of general objection. The dispensation also obtained by the general objector is, to a large extent, offset by the disqualification that the general objector suffers from full participation in the political process. The general objector is opting for a sectarian separation from full political involvement.

There are implications as well, of course, for the principle that the law must support the common defense. As Professor Greenawalt suggests, the problem is not with endangering the power of the government to conscript or recruit adequate troops, but rather with the impact on military discipline and on the political resolve to fight, this latter impact flowing from skepticism about the rule of law and the equity of distributions. In the past, for most of history in fact, the Catholic Church has conceded that this balance of factors tilts against recognition of the SCO exemption. Why has the Church changed its judgment? I suggest a number of reasons, which may be read more or less clearly in the language of relevant church documents. They include:

1. The democratic process and democratic lawmakers may not be fully capable of the needed moral assessment of developing technologies. In a sense there is no one at the helm.
2. The framework for assessing the legitimacy of political action and law is increasingly *the international common good*. National actions that affect the international common good have only a provisional legality or validity. The presumption of legitimacy of national political decisions is in fact weaker.
3. Even to the degree that the political process can retain moral control over the state use of technology, this is a slow project. Media bring information to individuals with unprecedented speed and thoroughness. Thus, it is far more likely that pressing problems of conscience will be generated for individuals, and more violations of individual moral integrity, where no exemption exists.
4. The moral gravity of the misuse of war technology is unprecedented. Immoral wars and means of waging war can do disproportionate damage: the consequences of a single immoral political decision could entail the destruction of the human race and even the biosphere. Again, grave qualms of individual conscience become much greater, and the threat of the violation of individual moral integrity more ubiquitous.

I agree with the bishops that some combination of these factors indeed tilts in favor of acknowledgment of the SCO exemption, assuming only that the appropriate form of accommodation can be found. Therefore, I agree with Professor Greenawalt with respect to the result: we both agree that accommodation should be made. I disagree with him however in the basis of justification I would give for the accommodation. It would be justification in a strong sense, based not on autonomy of choice but on respect for the value of individual moral integrity.

The Appropriate Form of Accommodation

Turning from the why of justification to the how of accommodation, I agree with Professor Greenawalt that the form of accommodation is a decisive question. He is correct that distributive justice requires that added burdens be substituted for burdens escaped by virtue of the exemption.

Moreover, the principle of respect for the rule of law requires that, symbolically, the objector be subjected to the law's coercive power in a way which is equally invasive of his or her freedom, in kind and degree, as that suffered by nonobjectors. Therefore, as far as possible, a militarized form of in-service alternative assignment should be favored as should a process for handling SCO applications within the ordinary military bureaucracy, assuming that the military could do this in good faith. Ideally, the military could analyze its operations in ways that allowed units to be designated nuclear and nonnuclear, domestic defense and foreign operations. As far as possible, objectors should be treated as fully competent soldiers who are expected to comply with military discipline and the chain of command in useful ways in the alternative assignment area. In many circumstances, the new assignment might involve no reduced, in fact an increased, burden or risk.

If the military cannot create such sanitized units anticipating the major lines of objection, then it should create segregated units for objectors only. These too should be as military as possible in use and application. Where the military found that it could not use a given objector at all, then a civilian work corps that functioned in a regimented fashion could be used for alternate assignments.

On the question of the form of accommodation, my most important disagreement with Professor Greenawalt is with his suggestion that the exemption be assigned on a no-fault administrative basis. I favor retention of formal classification based on conscientious claim. With respect to in-service selective objection (which, after all, is an integral part of the bishops' proposal), Professor Greenawalt's proposed alternative would be far more disruptive of military discipline. Namely, the military would be allowing its entire corps of personnel free to opt out of assignments at will, assuming only a willingness to take a longer tour of duty in another area. Restricting the option to conscientious claimants would restrict the number of applicants and it would justify giving them the freedom in question in terms of a higher duty which cross-validates the duty to obey military commands.

In addition, even with pre-induction accommodation, there are serious difficulties with Professor Greenawalt's proposal. While it involves perhaps less paperwork, I believe that it is the more bureaucratic option. It is faceless and does not require accountability. It does not vindicate the value of moral integrity, but rather, at most, autonomy of choice, a value which does not justify the exemption. By not requiring individuals to account for the conscientious nature of their positions, it deprives lawmakers of a valuable witness of assistance in their own separate ongoing analysis of the morality of state action.

This no-fault approach also trivializes military service, which should itself be understood as a response to moral obligation. Given this system of no-fault options, military service would become a matter of personality characteristics, such as how risk-prone or risk-averse the individual is, along with correlated aspects of social status. Death or other serious harm suffered by reasons of military service is far more palatable if it is seen as a badge of having done a moral duty well, than if it is seen as the consequence of a self-interested gamble.

Although Professor Greenawalt's analysis of the problems with a classification system is largely cogent, the problems he stipulates can be solved by modifying the system of classification and not abandoning it. I agree that the "religious" requirement should be dropped, for instance in keeping with *Welsh v. United States* and *United States v. Seeger*. The religious training and belief issue is really a test of both sincerity and conscientiousness. There are many other available indicia of these qualities. The Catholic bishops seek to uphold integrity of conscience which is a concern for all human beings, whether or not religious.[7] So, they do not require this criterion.

There is a special danger of bias in administering an SCO exemption based on classification. This would be particularly true if the bishops' just-war form of moral analysis was made normative. Middle-class people who memorized an idiosyncratic form of argumentation would be favored. The requirements for SCO classification should be limited to sincerity and conscientiousness.

In this context, I disagree with Professor Greenawalt's definition of conscientiousness. The willingness to accept martyrdom is a validation of sincerity, rather than a test of conscientiousness. The conscientious claim should be defined as one based on a belief that participation would result in a grave violation of individual moral integrity. Political disagreement or even moral disapproval of state action would not be sufficient.

The exemption would be granted once a prima facie case was established, barring evidence to the contrary. Compensatory burdens and symbolic forms of control over the objector would keep the system in check. Naturally, military exigencies would place further requirements on the time, place, and manner of applications.

In summary, I favor accommodation that is justified in the strong sense that I have explained and which involves a test of sincerity and conscientiousness, as well as compensatory burdens on, and symbolic governmental control over, the individual. Professor Greenawalt seeks another form of accommodation with another kind of justification. His proposal emerged from the practical crucible of the Vietnam debate and there is reason to think that his proposal is more likely to be accepted than are the alternatives I propose.

Notes

1. Washington, D.C.: United States Catholic Conference.
2. Washington, D.C.: National Conference of Catholic Bishops.
3. 406 U.S. 205 (1982).
4. 401 U.S. 437 (1971).
5. 455 U.S. 252 (1982).
6. United States Catholic Conference, *Economic Justice for All: Catholic Social Teaching and the U.S. Economy* (1986).
7. See Vatican Council II's "Declaration of Religious Freedom," *The Documents of Vatican II*, Walter Abbott and Joseph Gallagher, eds. (N.Y.: American Press, 1966), p. 1.

3

Selective Service and
the Conscientious Objector

George Q. Flynn

In the spring of 1941, when draftees reported to their local boards in Chicago, they were offered a prayer book. Vincent L. Knaus, chairman of an advisory board to Selective Service, wrote with pride to President Franklin Roosevelt that the Knights of Columbus had begun to distribute copies of *My Sunday Missal* to draft registrants. Paul G. Armstrong, state draft director, thought the distribution was "great work."[1] Selective Service was always aware of the importance of religion, because some churches rejected war and the draft on grounds of conscientious objection. The following pages trace the history of how the state sought to deal with this intractable problem.

The conscientious objector (CO) existed before the state but up to 1917 presented only a minor problem because there was no national draft. But with the arrival of mass armies and a national draft in the 20th century, new arrangements had to be made. The Conscription Act of 1917 erected a CO system elaborate in detail and narrow in focus. The Act required registration of all males in the eligible age group. If a man claimed CO status he had to prove membership in an established peace church. These churches included Quakers, Mennonites, Brethren and Friends, who all taught a pacifist creed. Even if classified a CO, he could still be drafted, but, after entering the armed forces, was eligible for noncombat service. Refusal to accept noncombat duty led to a court-martial and perhaps jail.[2]

The formal requirements proved unworkable. In December, 1917, the Army told draft boards to offer CO status to men who based their claim merely upon personal scruples. The drafted CO who refused noncombat duty now became eligible for alternate work designated by the president. Some 56,830 men were recognized as CO's but only 29,000 were physically qualified to serve and only 21,000 were inducted for noncombat duty. Another 4,000 refused military duty.

These totals represented a small fraction of the 3 million men inducted, but the principles in the law and the problems in practical application had caused confusion which led to modifications through executive and administrative orders. This pattern returned in World War II.[3]

By 1940 the Roosevelt administration had begun a timid mobilization. A peacetime conscription bill appeared in Congress under sponsorship of Grenville Clark and other veterans of the preparedness movement of 1915.[4] Roosevelt lagged behind in supporting the bill because White House surveys reported considerable draft opposition among labor unions, educational institutions, and churches. Representatives of peace churches had approached Roosevelt as early as 1937, calling for special protection for CO's in any draft. Any new draft bill had to deal with this issue.[5]

The War Department acted to revise the Clark bill to fit its own plans. Since the mid-1920s a special Joint Army Navy Selective Service Committee (JANSSC) had been drafting plans for conscription. Under the leadership of Major Lewis B. Hershey, the JANSSC now offered a system of dealing with CO's. As the World War I law, this plan recognized CO's only as members of established peace churches. But in contrast to 1917, the new plan provided for dealing with CO's before induction. Two basic categories were established: I-A-O for those willing to serve in noncombat military roles, and I-O for those refusing all military service. The classification and assignment of CO's fell under the authority of local draft boards and an appeal system was provided within Selective Service.

Peace church lobbyists, led by Paul Comly French and Raymond Wilson, challenged these provisions. French and others argued with Selective Service and Congress that some recognition should be granted the absolute pacifist who refused to serve in either the military or in alternate work. In addition, the lobbyists tried to establish individual conscience rather than church membership as the basis for the classification. Finally, they wanted civilians, preferably the Department of Justice, to control the appeal system.[6]

Selective Service officials compromised on many of these issues. Hershey was happy to allow the Justice Department a larger role. He also agreed that the focus should be on the individual. Church membership was dropped as a requirement. French came away from meetings convinced that Hershey had no intention of jailing CO's and would protect those sincerely opposed to war. But, reflecting public opinion and a pessimistic view of human nature, Selective Service and Congress insisted that there be some religious basis for a claim, that a man must reject all war rather than particular ones, and that the CO perform some alternate service.[7]

The final draft of the bill offered some satisfaction to the peace lobbyists, although they failed to achieve their full program. The Department of Justice eventually dodged the responsibility for appeals. A Justice official would act as a hearing officer on appeals but final authority remained within Selective Service, through state and presidential boards. Selective conscientious objection was rejected and the basis of the classification had to be "religious training and belief," but one did not have to be a member of a peace church. There was to be no imprisonment of CO's who refused noncombat service. They were required to perform alternate service under a program established by presidential regulations. The law fell short of French's aims, but it still represented a considerable improvement over World War I.[8]

Other problems arose over drafting and implementing regulations. In the midst of calling up millions of men Selective Service had little time for dealing with CO's. The system was decentralized, and local boards were staffed with patriotic civilians. When French and Wilson met with Hershey to discuss proposed regulations, however, there was harmony and good will on both sides. The task of devising a system of alternate service for those who refused noncombat duty was delegated by the president to Selective Service, which turned much of the job over to the peace churches, through the National Service Board of Religious Objectors (NSBRO).[9]

Throughout the country men shared similar experiences. When a CO registered he filed a form which indicated that he had objections of conscience. His local board then sent him an additional form upon which he elaborated on his objection, indicating church affiliation and other background information to assist the board in an evaluation of his sincerity. In general, local board members had little familiarity with ethical problems and little respect for pacifism. The main task of the local board was to fill calls for the armed forces. In classifying the men, the board first weeded out the physically and mentally unfit, and offered deferments for reasons of occupation and family status. Only if the CO could not be excused for other reasons was he considered for I-O or I-A-O.[10]

Assigning such a classification was a challenging task. Board members tried to determine the sincerity of conscience in a pluralistic society. The board's natural tendency was to take the easy way and focus upon church membership as the sine qua non of CO classification. But Clarence Dykstra, the first Director of Selective Service, instructed local boards that "judgment of individual conscience," independent of church membership should be recognized. The Department of Justice also informed Selective Service that the term "religious belief" could "include all shades of opinion and conviction, ranging from denial of God to adherence to dogmas." The right of conscience included individual belief or disbelief in the supernatural. The guiding norm became the sincerity of individual conviction, not formal adherence to a creed.[11]

The struggle to have local boards accept a broad definition continued throughout the war. Hershey, who replaced Dykstra as Director, emphasized that there should be a supernatural source for beliefs, but affirmed that the focus should remain on the individual. When local boards requested clear guidelines to help them, national headquarters insisted that defining religious training and belief was "too fundamental to try to lay down guides by which to test." But Hershey insisted that "it is general policy to show leniency in the handling of conscientious objectors and it is not necessary that conscientious objector be a member." If the individual rejected all wars and had a history of following such a precept in peace, rather than adopting it after receiving his draft notice, he should be given the benefit of doubt, no matter how unorthodox his "religion."[12]

Attempting to mitigate injustice, Congress and Selective Service erected an elaborate appeals system. In establishing his status the CO was first entitled to a personal hearing by the local board. If the local board refused the claimant's reclassification, he could appeal to a state board, which meant an automatic hearing before an official of the Department of Justice. The hearing officer then made a recommendation to the state appeal board which voted to uphold or reverse the local board. If denied at the state level, a registrant could appeal to the Federal level.[13]

Although staffed by military officers and headed by General Hershey, the presidential board insisted that "if a man's experience in the world leads him to a sincere conviction that he may not participate . . . in war, it cannot be maintained that his conviction is invalid because he arrived at it along other than accepted and defined paths of religious training." The infinite variety of religious experience in the United States was cited for broadening the term.[14]

Many local board rejections were overturned upon appeal. Hearings by the Justice Department resulted in overturning local board rejections in sixty-five percent of all appeal cases. At the presidential level an even more liberalizing effect occurred. The presidential board sustained local board classifications in only one out of five appeals. Peace church representatives admitted that CO appeals were given serious and careful attention by Selective Service.[15]

Less satisfying than the appeal system were the provisions for alternate service. After establishing his right to a CO classification, an individual was required to engage in work of national importance as specified by the president. In fact, the president had little to do with the program. In hopes of gaining some control over CO treatment, the peace churches offered to staff and finance the program. Hershey accepted this offer but his idea of equivalency of sacrifice insured that men were sent to public service camps at former Civilian Conservation Corps stations. Selective Service organized camps for almost 12,000 CO's during the war. Peace church funding saved the government money, but Selective Service maintained overall control of the camps. Pacifists' leaders later insisted that they had been misled about the program.[16]

In fact, no one was happy with the camps. Even with alternate service, the CO risked physical violence from red-blooded and red-necked patriots. Selective Service officials constantly complained at the messy way the camps were run. Reports indicated that the men loafed around, discussed philosophy and rejected any discipline. The CO's objected because the camps were under the final authority of military men and the work was not of national importance.[17]

Despite good will on both sides, wartime mobilization was so vast, the bureaucracy so elaborate and the nation so individualistic, that conflicts were unavoidable. Selective Service officials saw their responsibility as rapidly filling military calls. National headquarters wanted the willing cooperation of all CO's. Selective Service used legal prosecution only as a last resort because nothing was gained from sending draft resisters to prison.[18]

But some did go to prison. The law required that all men in the liable age group had to register with the draft. If inducted, the individual was obligated to report for examination, and if found suitable, enter the service. Yet some CO's refused to register and rejected any dealings with the draft system. These individuals were reported to the F.B.I., prosecuted, and imprisoned. In prison, the warden signed their registration cards. When they finished their sentence they were again liable for the draft and could be rearrested, reconvicted, and imprisoned again. Other signs of resistance emerged in the public service camps, through refusal to do assigned work, or even to report to the camps.[19]

After the war the Department of Justice reported a high level of conformity to conscription. Some 31.5 million men were registered and about 10 million were inducted. About 15 million men were called up to meet induction needs, but only 361,101 cases of suspected delinquency emerged and only 15,758 convictions resulted. This represented less than one-tenth of one percent of all registrants, a smaller ratio than during World War I. Of the 15,758 convictions only about 6,000 involved CO's. Of the 6,000 some three-fourths involved Jehovah Witnesses, who presented unique problems not easily related to conscientious objection.[20]

A program covering so many different individuals and dealing with something as sensitive as conscience had to provoke a variety of evaluations. After the War both sides had recommendations for changes in any future program. The peace churches criticized the camp operation and insisted that CO's be given the same pay as enlisted men. They wanted the entire program to be run by civilians and wanted alternate work more in line with "national importance."[21]

From a state perspective the program seemed a success. Selective Service was able to draft ten million men without creating martyrs of conscience. Some 25,000 CO's served in noncombat assignments and 12,000 participated in alternate work programs. The number of inductees had tripled from World War I, but the number of draft evaders only doubled. Having based a decentralized draft upon the strength of peer pressure and public relations, Selective Service officials were pleased with the results. Although they complained at the time spent on the few CO's, local board officials gave the program an 80 percent approval rating after the war. The public also endorsed the program.[22] Selective Service had achieved its objective of filling military wants while avoiding public disunity or criticism. The CO was handled outside of military law. The categories of objection were broadened and in practice included nonorthodox or nonchurched CO's, although "religious training and belief" remained an official requirement. Social and political objections remained inexcusable, as did selective conscientious objection.[23]

After the war Congress called for the end of conscription, but the Truman administration needed manpower to fulfill garrison obligations. Finally, in 1947, the armed forces decided to rely on volunteers, President Truman called for Universal Military Training (UMT) and the draft ended. One year later, UMT being sidetracked by Congress and volunteers being scarce, Truman called for a renewal of the draft to meet the postwar rivalry of the Soviet Union. In the new draft proposal the Congress again recognized the role of religion and conscience in society.

During debate on the bill congressmen accepted several recommendations by General Hershey.[24] He called for pay for CO's in any alternate service program, but he had no desire to deal directly with this "contentious" group. The absence of a fighting war and Hershey's World War II experience helped shape the new CO requirements. If recognized by the Selective Service as being a CO, a man was granted an absolute excuse from all duty. He could still request noncombat duty, but otherwise he received a deferment without alternate work. The new law also changed the definition of CO by accepting Hershey's working definition and defining "religious training and belief" as meaning "an individual's belief in a relation to a Supreme Being involving duties superior to those arising from any human relations, but does not include essentially political, sociological, or philosophical views or a merely personal moral code." Finally, following the critique of the NSBRO, the law established a new all-civilian presidential appeal board, independent of Selective Service headquarters.[25]

Once again draft registration began across the country and men faced problems of conscience. But Selective Service had few problems. The United States was officially at peace and the draft was used merely to stimulate voluntary enlistments. Indeed, draft calls dropped to zero by early 1949. The absolute deferment offered CO's was accepted by a nation at peace. Up to June 1950 almost 7.8 million men were classified by the draft. Of this group only about 10,000 claimed CO status and this included those who were willing to serve in noncombat jobs. The key ingredient in this congenial atmosphere, however, was peace, which proved transitory.[26]

On June 25, 1950, North Korean troops pushed across an artificial border into South Korea. President Truman read this action as a test of American determination to contain communism. Acting rapidly, but with the enthusiastic support from public opinion, Truman soon had the U.S. fighting in Korea under United Nations auspices. This intervention came at a critical time for Selective Service. Even as North Korean troops pushed south, Congress debated whether to extend a draft which had seemed redundant because it failed to draft anyone. Truman's response to the Korean war now insured a continued need for the drafts. As a temporary step, Congress extended the provisions of 1948 for another year.[27]

Draft calls increased rapidly and by January, 1951, some 220,000 had been inducted. The public soon became less tolerant of an absolute deferment for CO's. The American Legion began a campaign to require alternate service. Letters arrived at state and national headquarters of Selective Service promoting the idea. In Montana a local board resigned in protest over the absolute deferment of CO's. Pressure emerged because of the casualties in Korea and the general climate of anti-communism. In early 1951, as Congress considered a draft renewal, the issue of CO status arose in both houses. Selective Service, anticipating problems, urged the NSBRO to come up with an alternate service plan.[28] The 1951 Draft Act, as signed by Truman on 19 June, reiterated most of the provisions of 1948 law but added that CO's found opposed to both combatant and noncombatant service should be assigned by local boards to work of national importance. The details of the operation were left to presidential regulations.[29]

Selective Service began drafting regulations for alternate service in late 1951. At first Hershey hoped to have another agency run the program, but he soon discovered that no other agency was interested. Again Selective Service established liaison with the American Friends Service Committee and the NSBRO. While unable to satisfy all their needs, the regulations did provide for voluntary assignment, for comparable pay and for nonprofit work. An executive order was issued on February 20, 1952. Roger Jones of the Bureau of the Budget predicted that the peace groups could work out all problems with Hershey.[30]

Hershey needed the peace churches because Congress turned down his request for a $150,000 supplemental appropriation and federal agencies showed little interest in hiring CO's. He finally asked the peace churches to come up with employment suggestions. After being classified, the CO submitted three possible jobs to his local board and the Selective Service picked a suitable one. If disagreement arose, the CO could appeal through state headquarters to an independent national board. The assignment was for 24 months, rather than the duration of the war as in World War II.[31]

The lessons of World War II were implemented in the new draft law and helped create a more acceptable system. The new work arrangements deflected opposition. Rather than a government camp, the CO was offered an individual work assignment, with equal pay. The work itself, selected by the CO, provided satisfaction for the humanitarian and spiritual ambitions of the individual. Men worked in hospitals and health programs, in the U.S. and abroad. According to official Selective Service figures, by the end of fiscal year 1955 there were 3,277 men assigned to I-W (special work) and 2,439 had completed their tour in such work. Given a total of 16,153,861 living registrants, the CO ratio seemed about the same as in World War II. A comparison with World War II figures may be dubious, given the new definition in the law, new regulations, and the absence of any alternate service until mid-1952, but there seemed to be neither a surge nor a serious decline in the CO witness during the Korean war.[32]

By January 31, 1961 a total of 10,937 CO's had been assigned, worked and finished their duty. From 1951 to 1961 only 16,616 men were classified as CO's. Selective Service estimated that only one in every 850 classified men was designated as a CO.[33] The Bureau of Prisons reported that only 206 pacifists were sentenced by the courts during the Korean War. This figure again includes the Jehovah Witnesses who continued to present problems by refusing to accept any work assignment.[34]

Stauffer Curry of the NSBRO council praised the new system.[35] But even with the changes most peace churches still regarded the operation as a necessary evil. The public still demanded some alternate work and showed little increase in tolerance for CO's. Similarly, the courts provided no relief from the theistic definition of a CO embodied in the draft law.[36]

The rules governing the CO program remained in place until the Vietnam War. A CO was entitled to an automatic hearing on his classification, even if the local board granted his claim. Like other registrants, he was considered for all lower deferred categories before facing the alternate service requirement. A CO who was married, or in school, or physically unfit, or in a defense job might never be classified as I.O. The alternate job had to take the man away from home, and he could not be hired in lieu of a nondraftable man. Although entitled to the going wage in the job, the CO was denied dependent and G.I. benefits. Refusal to take an assignment led to prosecution.[37] The law required that beliefs be associated with a Supreme Being. But practically, a system had emerged which offered many deferment opportunities and allowed the CO to engaged in humanitarian work of his own choosing.

By 1954 the Korean conflict had degenerated into an armed truce due to the death of Stalin and diplomacy of Eisenhower. Draft calls began falling in the summer of 1953. In 1954 calls were never higher than 23,000 per month and they continued to decline throughout the Eisenhower presidency.[38] This period of draft doldrums coincided with a new defense strategy, which downgraded army manpower and upgraded air force hardware. Given this reduction in need for men, the draft reverted once again to a secondary role of stimulating volunteers for the armed forces. Even with the reduction of calls, an embarrassing surplus of men reached eighteen each year. With calls low and the draft age cohort increasing yearly, Hershey admitted that there was little concern over the CO's. Selective Service began erecting an elaborate system of scientific and educational deferments. With the myriad opportunities to gain a deferment, the I-O and I-W classifications never rose over .05 percent of all classifications.[39] But this scene could change rapidly if draft calls rose, and if draftees began dying on distant battlefields.

With the Vietnam War these conditions were met and America's tolerance of conscience was again tested. As a Lutheran spokesman wrote: "The experience of Vietnam taught many Americans that it is no longer possible to place conscience and political responsibility in separate compartments."[40] In 1964 draft calls dropped to only 4,900 in September. All college males were deferred. But on 28 July 1965 President Johnson decided to increase the commitment of American ground troops to the war in Vietnam and turned to the draft to find the men. Calls were doubled from 17,000 to 35,000 a month beginning in August.[41] The draft law, renewed every four years after 1951, still required military service from all able-bodied males from age 19 to 26. The CO provisions of the law had remained unchanged after 1951. The American public accepted this system. In May 1965, a Gallup poll of male college students found 61 percent favoring a continuation of the draft and only 37 percent favoring an all volunteer force. College women favored continuation by 76 percent.[42]

But in March 1965, even before Johnson's decision to expand the draft, some college males began demonstrating against the war. The anti-war protest movement, which started in 1965, grew in intensity over the next several years and reached a crescendo under President Nixon. Rooted in such disparate factors as disillusionment following the Kennedy assassination, the Civil Rights movement, an identity crisis of youth, religious enthusiasm and anti-establishment rebellion, the anti-war protest soon became an anti-draft movement. The draft was a tangible and easily reached symbol of involvement.[43]

The rise of anti-war protest had many consequences, not the least of which was helping to unseat a president. From the point of view of conscientious objection, the movement's most important impact was to blur the distinction between pacifists and non-pacifists. The existing legal requirements for CO status quickly became inadequate. The problem of how to identify a CO became an issue of public debate. Especially troublesome for Selective Service was pressure to recognize that a man might qualify for CO status if he objected only to war in Vietnam. Selective conscientious objection was not recognized in the law, but laws can be changed, especially when the existing system begins to malfunction.[44]

Identifying the CO had always been difficult. Now, during Vietnam, the task became almost impossible. The traditional CO organizations offered counsel to those who wished to be classified I.O.[45] By 1966 their services were inundated with new converts. Arlo Tatum, director of the Central Committee for CO's, admitted the impossibility of distinguishing in a short interview a man's hostility toward war from hostility to the draft. One lawyer, who specialized in defending draft delinquents, confessed that most CO claims centered on opposition to the war in Vietnam. Even Roman Catholics, who had no tradition of pacifism and had never constituted a large segment of CO claims, now applied in large numbers. In April 1967 Martin Luther King urged his civil rights followers to seek exemption from the draft by becoming CO's. Father Phillip Berrigan poured duck blood over the files of a Baltimore Selective service office, and one thousand seminarians wrote Secretary of Defense Robert McNamara demanding CO recognition against participation in the particular war in Southeast Asia.[46]

The issue of selective conscientious objection laid bare the tension between theory and practice in the draft. If the key determinant to obtaining CO status was to be conscience, rather than dogma or ritual, and if conscience by its very nature was particular and individualistic, then selective conscientious objection seemed only logical. Indeed, Selective Service had used individual sincerity as the test in the past. Religious leaders now began stressing this logic. In 1967 American religious organizations fell in line behind selective CO's By 1969 the United Church of Christ, the Lutherans, the Episcopal Church, the National Council of Churches of Christ, the Rabbinical Assembly and the Roman Catholic Bishops had all gone on record as supporting selective conscientious objection.[47]

A conflict emerged between an intellectual or philosophical concept of morality and the prudential concerns about mobilizing men for war. The attempt to balance the interest between the individual conscience and the nation's needs had been going on since the origins of the state and since 1940 for Selective Service. The selective CO merely made the problem more theoretical. If legitimate authority condoned the war and controlled information on it, how could an individual decide ethical issues? Did the government deserve any benefit of doubt? If every man could decide for himself whether to serve, planning for defense might become impossible. If individual conscience alone could justify CO status, what screening could be devised to insure that the privilege was not abused?[48]

In 1965 the courts offered some help with new interpretations on how the system should define a CO. The Supreme Court, in the case of *U.S. v. Seeger*, spoke to the legality of requiring that conscience be related to religious training and belief. Congress had sought to strengthen this association in 1948 by including in the law a reference to a "Supreme Being." Seeger, an agnostic, failed to qualify, but argued that his ethical creed should be sufficient.

The Court agreed. Although upholding the constitutionality of the CO provision, Justice Tom Clark, writing for the Court, defined "Supreme Being" and "religious training" in a broad manner. Clark insisted that the deciding factor was whether or not the man's beliefs occupied a place comparable to that occupied by traditional religion. If the belief did so function such ideas could not be rejected because they were incomprehensible to draft officials. The task of the local board was limited to deciding if the registrant's beliefs were sincerely held "and [were] in his own scheme of things, religious." Clark insisted that a moral code had to be clearly stated as merely personal to disqualify the claimant.[49]

Hershey informed the local boards of the Court's decision, but this hardly prevented confusion. The boards had always attempted to measure sincerity rather than just orthodoxy, but members had relied upon traditional concepts of religion.

Now the Court had stripped the deity from religion and left local boards the task of measuring sincerity. Past behavior and witnesses were still helpful, but distinguishing between "essentially political, sociological, or philosophical views or a merely personal moral code," which did not qualify under the law, and "religious training and belief," which did qualify, became more difficult.[50]

By 1966 protest against the Vietnam War reached the point of mass demonstrations. Students sat in draft offices, destroyed records, burned their draft cards. This protest led President Johnson, in July, to appoint a National Advisory Commission on Selective Service, headed by Burke Marshall. Congress, not to be upstaged, established its own investigation under General Mark Clark.

The issue of selective CO's received particular attention in the Marshall study. Fr. John Courtney Murray, a leading Catholic theologian, and Kingman Brewster, president of Yale, both members of the panel, favored the idea. Murray insisted that the current law, requiring opposition to all wars, violated the Catholic-Christian theory of just wars. This theory had been developed more to guide leaders than draftees, but Fr. Murray applied it in 1967 and found the moral premise of the Vietnam war was "absolutely indefensible."[51] Despite his efforts, however, neither the Marshall Commission report, nor the Clark report in 1967 supported selective CO's. The two studies disagreed on many aspects of the draft, but did agree that the current CO policy of the system should remain unchanged.[52]

The war and the protest continued as Congress began deliberations in the summer of 1967 on renewing induction authority. Those expecting a liberalization of the CO provisions of the law were to be disappointed. A backlash had developed in the country against the anti-war movement. Polls indicated that 59 percent of the public believed the US role in Vietnam was "morally justified." A law had passed making it a felony to burn one's draft card.[53] Congress was in no mood to coddle protesters.

As hearings began on the new draft bill, the momentum was toward tightening up deferments and getting tough with protesters and draft dodgers. Representative F. Edward Hebert complained that the Justice Department paid too much attention to the First Amendment. Mrs. J. Robert Reynolds, secretary of the Unitarian Universalist Association, faced long odds when she offered to Congress a resolution calling for a broader concept of the CO, including ethical and moral grounds and selective objection. Congress was more receptive to the testimony of General Clark. Clark testified that the *Seeger* decision meant each man could decide for himself if he wished to fight. In short order the House Armed Services Committee drafted a new provision which struck out the term "Supreme Being," but kept the requirement that the claim had to be "by reason of religious training and belief." In a direct message to the Supreme Court, the new law stated that religious training and belief "does not include essentially political, sociological, or philosophical views, or a merely personal moral code."[54]

The new law rejected the reforms suggested by the Marshall Commission and even eliminated a provision for automatically referring all CO claims to the Justice Department. Now a delinquent CO could be accelerated for induction just like any other draftee. The new terminology also sent a message to local boards that narrow rather than broad definitions were the order of the day.[55]

Because of the decentralized character of the draft system it is risky to make generalizations about board treatment of CO's. Staffing principles remained consistent; the same veterans and patriots, now much older, predominated, although under President Johnson's prodding more minorities were appointed. Hershey again reminded boards of the need for tolerance. But inconsistencies in treatment continued to arise. After the mandatory hearing requirement was eliminated, Hershey revised procedures so that the local board was required to invite the CO for a talk, hopefully to promote mutual understanding. At these discussions some board members resented the uniformity of CO responses, which was attributed to counseling by anti-war groups. Officially, national headquarters insisted that opposition to a particular war was political and disqualifying. But, as in the past, an individual's sincerity could overcome the letter of the law.[56]

From 1964 to June 1973 the Army issued calls for 1,903,230 men. The system responded by delivering 2,338,819 men to induction centers, where 1,918,364 were finally inducted. CO claims failed to interfere with the functioning of the draft. During this period a total of 144,807 men were classified as I-O and 70,550 assumed alternate work assignments. The CO's represented the smallest deferred class. In mid-1964 about six of every 10,000 registrants were classified as CO's. By 1970 the rate had grown to ten out of 10,000, still a lower rate than the 1950s. In 1971, 34,203 men were classified as CO's, the high figure for the entire period. By 1972 the total slipped to 16,071 and continued to decline.[57]

The alternate work program for those classified I-O remained the same as during the Korean War. From 1965 to 1967 the number in I-W almost tripled in volume, jumping from 2,351 to 6,166. Yet until 1968 the system adjusted well and found an adequate number of employment opportunities.[58]

Upon assuming office in 1969, President Nixon tried to end the draft and Vietnamize the war. He soon adopted a lottery system for the draft and replaced Hershey with Curtis Tarr. Tarr asked local board members to assure themselves that the registrant was not acting merely from expediency. Although the registrant need not believe in a traditional God, he did have to hold his beliefs "with the strength of traditional religious conviction." Only those men whose beliefs were "not deeply held," and those whose objection to war rested upon "pragmatism or expediency," could be denied a CO classification.[59]

By the end of 1970, Nixon had begun moving toward an all-volunteer force. Draft calls were cut as Vietnamization went into effect. CO claims increased and Tarr admitted that the court decisions had probably influenced local boards "to classify more of those who do apply into I-O."[60] The last draft calls were made in the spring of 1973. American churches applauded this decision. Although the All-Volunteer Army had problems, the CO was not one of them.

The issue arose again, however, on June 27, 1980, when President Jimmy Carter, in a response to the Soviet invasion of Afghanistan, obtained congressional authority to register 19 and 20 year-old men. The new registration hardly began when the Central Committee for CO's announced a revival of counseling work. Protest against the draft also appeared, although no inductions were authorized by Congress. A Gallup poll of June 1980 indicated that 80 percent of the public favored registration; even 66 percent of the draft age population approved the idea. But only 58 percent approved the return of induction, and in the draftable ages, only 37 percent. As the principles guiding CO treatment remained those established by the 1967 law, recognition of conscience continued to be a matter of concern.[61]

Since 1917 the law has required that conscience be expressed in some measurable form, initially by membership in a church. In practice, however, this requirement proved impractical. To protect conscience the government focused upon the sincerity of the individual in his beliefs. This practical solution failed to satisfy those defending the right of conscience. Raymond Wilson of the Society of Friends was probably correct when he wrote after World War II that "there is no satisfactory solution for the problem of conscience under conscription—only a series of more or less unsatisfactory accommodations."[62]

Yet a review of CO treatment since 1917 offers some hope for reformers. From a World War I program restricted to members of peace churches and handled by the military, the nation moved to a broad definition which included agnostics and atheists. While initially considered a military problem, the CO became the responsibility of Selective Service and eventually was offered alternate work of his own choice. This evolution seems consistent with the experience of other western nations.[63]

The absence of inductions and war ensures a hypothetical context to any discussion of the recognition of the selective CO. Without question the Selective Service should be sympathetic to a proposal which would allow a man to declare himself a CO and be dropped from the rolls. Considering the small numbers involved, the CO classification has cost Selective Service an inordinate amount of time and controversy. The system's main responsibility is to find fighting men for the armed forces. Wrestling with CO's over definitions of religion and sincerity has generated much sweat but very few soldiers.

Yet the system functions within a political context. The CO exemption has been imposed by Congress and public opinion and reflects the fear of abuse. Our decentralized draft has always depended primarily upon peer pressure within local communities for enforcement. Given the assumptions and commitments of American foreign policy, a system of guaranteeing fighting manpower remains in standby condition. Currently, the all-volunteer system satisfies political and military needs. But even President Ronald Reagan, after rejecting it in the 1980 election, acknowledged the need for a draft registration.

In the present context, recognition in law of the selective CO may be possible. But the new surge of patriotism under an adventurous president has created a quite different political environment from the era of Vietnam.

Notes

1. Knaus to Roosevelt, 3 May 1941, OF 1413, Box 5, Franklin D. Roosevelt Papers, Roosevelt Library, Hyde Park, N.Y. (hereafter cited as FDR).

2. The conscientious objector (CO) had existed even before the state. Colonial militia regulations recognized him and offered some alternate form of service or contribution. Substitution or paying a fee remained a solution to the CO problem even when the first federal draft law was adopted in the Civil War. See Selective Service System, *Conscientious Objection*, Special Monograph No. 11, 2 vols. (Wash.: USGPO, 1950), I, 41; Judy Barrett, "The Conscientious Objector in America," in National Advisory Committee on Selective Service, box 56, Record Group (RG) 220, National Archives, Washington. A 1864 draft revision provided for alternate, noncombat service for the CO.

3. Charles Chatfield, *For Peace and Justice: Pacifism in America, 1914–1941* (Knoxville: U. of Tenn., 1971), pp. 68–70; J. Harold Sherk, "The Position of the Conscientious Objector," *Current History* (1968) 55: 19; R. R. Russell, "Development of Conscientious Objector Recognition in the United States," *George Washington Law Review* (1951–52), 20: 420, 430–31; S.S., *CO Monograph*, pp. 49, 54, 63.

4. J. Garry Clifford and Samuel R. Spencer, Jr., *The First Peacetime Draft* (Lawrence: Univ. Press of Kansas, 1986) provides details on the fight for this bill.

5. One survey of Catholic college students found 41 percent favoring conscription, but 36 percent declaring themselves conscientious objectors. Addison G. Foster to Lowell Mellett, 15 August 1940, OF 788 Box 3, FDR; Russell, "Development," pp. 412–3, 437; Msgr. M. Ready to Woodring, 25 November 1939, Box 24, Selective Service Records, RG 147–97, N.A.; E. Raymond Wilson, "Evolution of the C.O. Provisions in the 1940 Conscription Bill," *Quaker History* (1975), 64: 3; 3; Roosevelt to Archbishop Samuel A. Stritch, 24 August 1940, OF 1413, Box 4, FDR; Patricia McNeal, "Catholic Conscientious Objection During World War II," *Catholic Historical Review* (1975), 6: 224.

6. S.S., *CO Monograph*, pp. 4–5 67, 75, 141; Wilson, "Evolution," 8–9.

7. Clifford and Spencer, *Peacetime Draft*, p. 221; Mulford Q. Sibley & Philip E. Jacob, *Conscription of Conscience: The American State and the Conscientious Objector, 1940–1947* (Ithaca: Cornell, 1952), pp. 48, 51.

8. Chatfield, *For Peace*, p. 306; James Rowe to President, 4 October 1940, OF 1413, Box 1, FDR.

9. Wilson, "Evolution," p. 12.

10. Sibley & Jacob, *Conscription*, pp. 54, 58, 64; Research and Statistics memo, S.S., Vertical File 200S5, 12 September 1951, Lewis B. Hershey Papers, Military History Institute, Carlisle Barracks, Pa. (hereafter cited as LBH); S.S., *CO Monograph*, pp. 255, 262, 332. For Thomas Merton's experience in seeking a deferment see Michael Mott, *The Seven Mountains of Thomas Merton* (Boston: Houghton Mifflin, 1984), pp. 165–171.

11. Sibley and Jacob, *Conscription,* p. 68; Duggan memo for Holtzoff, 22 October 1940, Box 31, file 323.5, RG 147–97, N.A.

12. Sibley & Jacob, *Conscription,* pp. 68, 307–08, argues that Hershey's appointment led to an "erosion of tolerance," but this is exaggerated. See George Q. Flynn, "Lewis B. Hershey and the Conscience Objector: The World War II Experience", *Military Affairs* (February 1983), 47: 1–6; Linton M. Collins to Edward S. Shattuck, 22 March 1941, Box 31, file 323.5, RG 147–97, N.A.; John D. Langston to Morgan, 7 April 1941, ibid; quote from LB memo, digest, file E37A, vol. 1, ibid.; S.S., *CO Monograph,* pp. 141–42.

13. Sibley & Jacob, *Conscription,* pp. 61; 72; S.S., *CO Monograph,* pp. 140, 258.

14. Sibley & Jacob, *Conscription,* p. 79; S.S., *CO Monograph,* pp. 137, 144, 153; Francis Biddle to President, 3 March 1944, OF lll, FDR.

15. During the war the Justice Department handled 12,353 claims. About 989 cases on CO's reached the presidential level. In about 80 percent of the cases, the decision reversed a local board's I-A classification. In addition, Hershey took 191 cases on direct appeal and granted CO status in 60 percent of cases. The CO's only complaint was with the military character of the appeal boards, which seemed in violation of the law. Congress, however, met this objection in 1943 by revising the law to permit officers to serve. Special Selective Service Commission to Director, 5 May 1944, VF 345.1S22, LBH; Sibley & Jacob, *Conscription,* p. 76; S.S.; *CO Monograph,* pp. 144–46; Angell, Jones, Lawrence to President, 7 March 1944, VF 345.1S22, LBH; U.S. Dept. of Justice, *Annual Report,* 30 June 1946, pp. 22–24, in VF 345.1x1, LBH.

16. Hershey to S. L. Van Akin, 23 April 1941, Box 31, file 323.5, RG 147–97, N.A. The ratio of camp assignees per 1,000 of church membership was as follows: Christadelphians—49.4; Mennonites—40.3; Friends—9.6; Brethren—7.8; Jehovah Witness—7.1; Church of God—1.2. All other denominations had less than 1 per 1,000 members. In total numbers, Mennonites had 4,610, Brethren 1,468; Friends 902; Methodist, 845; Jehovah Witnesses, 532. The others were all under 300. See S.S., *CO Monograph,* p. 320.

17. Roger Juhnke, "The Perils of Conscientious Objection," *Mennonite Life,* September 1979, pp. 5–9, describes how a group of Kansas Mennonite CO's were tortured on the bus taking them to an examination station in 1944. Major Franklin A. McLean to Paul French, 13 October 1941, Box 31, file 323.5, RG 147–97, N.A.; Lewis F. Kosch to Hershey, 29 Oct. 1941, ibid; Kosch to French, 25 June 1941, ibid.

18. S.S., *CO Monograph,* pp. 257, 260; Special Commission to Director, 5 May 1944, VF 345.1522, LBH; Henry Stimson to Rep. Andrew J. May, 14 August 1945, Reel 360, item 5317, George C. Marshall Papers, V.M.I., Lexington, VA.

19. Hershey to Malvina Thompson, Series 70, Box 912, Eleanor Roosevelt Papers, FDR.

20. During World War II almost 4,000 Jehovah's Witnesses were convicted and sent to jail for violation of the draft law. About 2,500 refused induction orders and 1,500 refused to participate in alternate work assignments. Selective Service sought vainly to deal with this problem. At first the CO provisions seemed suitable for such men, but upon learning that qualification required rejecting all wars, the Jehovah's Witnesses demurred. They rejected pacifism because they saw themselves as God's warriors at Armageddon. Instead, they demanded ministerial exemptions. Exemptions were limited to members of the Bethel Family in Pennsylvania and men who distributed literature as a full-time job. When they were denied ministerial exemption and offered alternate work as CO's, many refused to cooperate. This attitude led to the prosecution and conviction of 4,000 members of the sect.

All the subtle distinctions in the regulations and the liberal interpretations offered by headquarters failed to prevent this problem. See Nathan T. Eliff, "Jehovah's Witnessess and the Selective Service Act," *Virginia Law Review* (September 1945), 31: 811–22; National Headquarters Opinions, 2 November 1942, E 42, vol. III, RG 147, N.A.; S.S., *CO Monograph*, p. 262; Chester J. Chastek to HQ, 9 June 1941; Box 31, Omer Reading File, RG 147–97, N.A.

In 1946, when President Truman's amnesty board looked over those imprisoned for draft violations, it found no justification for a general amnesty. As Owen Roberts, the Chair, wrote, a general amnesty would restore rights to many "who neither were, nor claimed to be, religious conscientious objectors." The commission had found that 50 percent of the cases indicated a prior record of more serious offenses. Report of President's Amnesty Board, 23 December 1946, Box 844, OF 245, Harry S. Truman Papers, Truman Library, Independence, Mo. (hereafter cited as HST).

The courts proved a modest hurdle to the effective execution of the draft system. In a series of decisions, the courts upheld the legality of the draft and the procedures of the Selective Service, including the alternative service program. There was some disagreement over defining the term "religious training and belief," and Justice A. Hand, in a circuit court decision, wrote that the court was willing to accept response to an inward mentor, or conscience, because this was the equivalent of a religious impulse. But there was no recognition of selective objectors. *Estep v. United States* 327 U.S. 114 (1946) and *Falbo v. United States,* 320 U.S. 549 (1944) established that judicial review of local board decisions was allowed only if the draftee had exhausted all administrative remedies and had refused the order to step forward at induction. Once he refused to step forward, he could seek a writ of habeas corpus. The constitutionality of the public service camps was upheld by *Roodenko v. United States,* 147 F.2nd 752 (10th Cir. 1944). In *United States v. Kauten,* 133 F.2d 703 (2d Cir. 1943) the Court concluded that Kauten's objection to the war was a political decision excluded by the statute. See James T. Connor, "Due Process and the Selective Service System," *Virginia Law Review* (June 1944), 30: 450–52; S.S., *Legal Aspects of Selective Service* (Wash: USGPO, 1969 rev.).

21. Ralph L. Lipscomb to Director, 17 February 1947, Box 59, RG 147–97, N.A.; A. S. Imirie to I. I. Denison, 25 July 1941, Box 30, ibid.

22. Memo from Ernest Angell, Rufus M. Jones, W. A. Lawrence to President, 7 March 1944, VF 345.1S22, LBH; Memo on Experience of American Friends Service Committee in Civilian Public Service under the Selective Service Act of 1940, n.d., VF 450.f, ibid.; Stuart W. Showalter, "American Magazine Coverage of Objectors to the Vietnam War," *Journalism Quarterly* (1976), 53: 649; Leo P. Crespi, "Attitudes Toward Conscientious Objectors and Some of Their Psychological Correlates," *The Journal of Psychology* (July 1944) 18: 115, who used only Princeton students in a survey. S.S., *CO Monograph,* p. 4, 105; Lawrence S. Wittner, *Rebels Against War: The American Peace Movement 1941–1960,* (N.Y.: Columbia, 1969), p. 42n.; Survey of Local Board Opinions, 1947, Box 62, RG 147–97, N.A.

23. Whittner, *Rebels,* pp. 41, 41n; S.S., *CO Monograph,* p. 1. Roman Catholics remained in limbo because of the absence of any doctrinal justification for total pacifism and the chauvinism of bishops. See McNeal, "Catholic CO's," pp. 226, 232. Only 122 Negroes claimed CO status during the war. See Report of Campbell Johnson to Director, 21 March 1947, Box 34, file 120.2, RG 147–97, N.A.

24. Paper on Ministerial Exemptions, by Neal M. Wherry, n.d., Box 59, File E97, RG 147, N.A. At a special experiment on Universal Military Training, conducted at Ft. Knox in 1948, a committee on religion acted to encourage all servicemen to attend church once each week. See "Report to President on Moral Safeguards for Trainees," 13 September 1948, Ent. 66, file 327.02, RG 330, N.A.

25. S.S., *Selective Service System Under the 1948 Act* (Wash.: USGPO, 1951), p. 31; Russell, "Developments," pp. 427, 435; Compton Committee Hearings, 18 April 1947, 1858, UMT, Box 12, HST; James M. Gerhardt, *The Draft and Public Policy* (Columbus: Ohio State U., 1971), p. 115.

26. Russell, "Development," p. 447; *S.S. Under 1948 Act*, p. 78.

27. Even Norman Thomas supported Truman's action. See Wittner, *Rebels,* pp. 201–03; George Q. Flynn, *Lewis B. Hershey, Mr. Selective Service* (Chapel Hill: U. of N.C., 1985) pp. 176–77.

28. Zelle A. Larson, "An Unbroken Witness: Conscientious Objection to War," unpublished Ph.D. dissertation, U. of Hawaii, 1975, pp. 158–61, 170–71; Flynn, Hershey, p. 177.

29. S.S., *Annual Report of the Director of Selective Service, 1951* (Wash.: USGPO, 1952), p. 1; Russell, "Development," p. 428.

30. Col. Grahl report, 19 May 1960, State Directors Conference (SDC), LBH; Roger W. Jones to Hopkins, 19 February 1952, OF 245, Box 845, HST.

31. *Selective Service* (Newsletter, hereafter cited as S.S.N.), July 1952, p. 1; S.S., *Annual Report of the Director of Selective Service, 1954* (Wash.: USGPO, 1955), p. 28; Larson, "Unbroken," pp. 190–92; J. E. Carroll to Gen. Vaughan, 15 September 1950, OF 440, Box 1288, HST.

32. S.S., *Annual Report of the Director of Selective Service, 1955* (Wash.: USGPO, 1956), p. 30; Stephen N. Kohn, *Jailed for Peace: The History of American Draft Law Violators, 1658–1985* (Westport: Greenwood, 1986), p. 70, uses a dubious methodology to conclude that in 1952 the percentage of inductees exempted as CO's had grown by ten times over the WW II rate. There was also a shift in the demographics of the CO movement. Whereas in World War II the majority of CO's sent to camps came from eastern, urban areas, during Korea a larger percentage of Mennonites served (67 percent compared to 40 percent earlier) and they came from rural, conservative areas. Larson, "Unbroken," pp. 290, 318.

33. The vast majority of those in the alternate service program were Mennonites, some 68 percent. Brethren and Friends groups provided another 15 percent. No other church or denomination supplied over 3 percent. From 1952 to 1965 only 38 Baptists and 12 Roman Catholics served, together with three members of the Church of the Four Leaf Clover. Almost all worked in hospitals—religious, private, county, and state. A few worked with private charity agencies and state social agencies. Nine CO's worked at the Fitzsimmons Army Hospital in Denver where they acted as volunteers to test the edibility of food exposed to atomic radiation. Less than 400 worked overseas in the institutions established by American peace churches. S.S., Research and Statistics Memo, 1 March 1961, VF 345, LBH: *Selective Service Statistics* vol. 4, pt. A, 31 Aug. 1961; ibid., 31 Jan. 1963; *S.S.,* Nov. 1954, p. 3; S.S. Fact sheet on CO's, 1952–1965, in Box 42, RG 220, N.A.; S.S., March 1966, p. 3.

34. Larson, "Unbroken," pp. 321–22, 98; S.S., *Annual Report of the Director of Selective Service, 1953* (Wash.: USGPO, 1954), p. 26; ibid., 1954, p. 28.

35. Larson, "Unbroken," pp. 194, 198.

36. George H. Gallup, comp., *The Gallup Poll: Public Opinion, 1935–1971*, 3 vols (N.Y.: Random House, 1972), II: 1124–5; See S.S.N., *Legal Aspects of Selective Service*, pp. 10–12, exp. *George v. United States*, 196 F.2d 445 (9th Cir. 1952) cert. den., 344 U.S. 843.

37. "CO Study," S.S. Research and Statistics Memo, 1 March 1961, VF 345, LBH; ibid., 1 March 1962. Selective Service did insist upon prosecution for men who refused to cooperate. From July 1952 through January 1961, only 900 men registered but refused to accept an alternate work assignment. Of this group, some 770 or 85 percent eventually did report. Of those who had to be prosecuted, the vast majority were members of the Jehovah's Witnesses. In such cases, Hershey sucessfully argued for continued prosecution if a man served an initial sentence. The law imposed an obligation which continued. The White House supported Hershey's position that only compliance with the CO program prevented continued prosecution. The courts also upheld this approach. While successful in this case, Hershey could not resolve the Jehovah's Witness problem. Many district courts began accepting all members as being entitled to ministerial exemptions. Hershey warned local boards that "We have to overcome our own prejudices," and "thank God we have our religious liberty and not go about trying to destroy others." The CO program simply did not work for Jehovah's Witnesses. S.S., Research and Statistics Memo, 1 March 1961, VF 345, LBH; Lyle Tatum to Gerald D. Morgan, 6 September 1955, Central file, OF, Box 664, Dwight D. Eisenhower Papers, Eisenhower Library, Abilene, Kansas (hereafter cited as DDE); Hershey to Gerald D. Morgan, 6 July 1955, ibid; J. William Barba to A. J. Muste and Ray Newton, 13 September 1955, ibid.; Russell, "Development," p. 440; quote in State Directors Conference, 16 May 1960, LBH.

38. S.S., *Annual Report of the Director of Selective Service, 1960* (Wash.: USGPO, 1961), p. 102.

39. S.S., *Annual Report, 1960*, pp. 90, 92.

40. Richard J. Niebanck, *Conscience, War and the Selective Objector*, 2d ed. (N.P.: Lutheran Church, 1972), p. 48. For America's entry into Vietnam see *The Pentagon Papers: The Senator Gravel Edition* (5 vols., Boston: Beacon Press, 1971–72); Guenter Lewy, *American in Vietnam* (N.Y.: Oxford, 1978); George C. Herring, *America's Longest War: The United States and Vietnam, 1950–1975* (N.Y.: Wiley, 1979). For the operation of the draft see Flynn, "Hershey," Sol Tax, ed., *The Draft: A Handbook of Facts and Alternatives* (Chicago: U. of Chicago, 1967); Lawrence M. Baskir & William A. Strauss, *Chance and Circumstance: The Draft, the War and the Vietnam Generation* (N.Y.: Knopf, 1978). For the protest movement see Michael Useem, *Conscription, Protest, and Social Conflict* (N.Y.: Wiley, 1973); Thomas Powers, *The War at Home: Vietnam and the American People, 1964–1968* (N.Y.: Grossman, 1973).

41. Flynn, *Hershey*, pp. 232–234.

42. Gallup Poll, 3: 1939.

43. For a discussion of the movement, see Irwin Unger, *The Movement: A History of the American New Left* (New York: Dodd, Mead, 1974) and Useem, *Conscription*.

44. Walter S. Griggs, Jr., "The Selective Conscientious Objector: A Vietnam Legacy," *Journal of Church and State* (1979), 21: 92.

45. Showalter, "American Magazines," pp. 650, 652; Kohn, *Jailed*, p. 126; Library of Congress, *U.S. Draft Policy* (Washington: USGPO, 1968), p. 15.

46. U.S., Congress, Senate, Subcommittee on Employment, Manpower and Poverty of the Committee on Labor and Public Welfare, *Hearings: Manpower Implications of Selective Service,* 90th Cong., 1st Session (April 6, 1987), pp. 249–260; Allan Brotsky, "Trial of a Conscientious Objector," in Ann F. Ginger, ed., *The Relevant Lawyers* (N.Y.: Simon & Schuster, 1972), p. 102; McNeal, "Catholic CO's," p. 222; Kohn, *Jailed,* p. 80; Charles E. Rice, "Conscientious Objection: A Conservative View," *Modern Age* (1968–69), 13: 67, 69; Robert P. Friedman and Charley Leistner, eds., *Compulsory Service Systems* (Columbia, MO: Artcraft Press, 1968), p. 368.

47. Griggs, "Selective CO's," pp. 95–7; Dean M. Kelly to Callard, 9 December 1969, Box 4, President's Committee on an All-Volunteer Force (PCAVF), RG 220, N.A.; Dean Dammann to Gates, 26 September 1969, ibid.

48. Griggs, "Selective CO," p. 98; Rice, "Conscientious Objection," pp. 68, 72; Peter J. Riga, "Selective Conscientious Objection: Progress Report," *The Catholic World* (1970), 211: 163. In *United States v. Sisson,* 297 F.Supp. 902 (D. Mass 1969), a district court in Massachusetts upheld Selective Conscientious Objection, because the judge felt the focus had to be on sincerity of conscience in a CO classification. But in 1971, in *Gillette v. United States,* 401 U.S. 437 (1971), this decision was reversed by the Supreme Court which also rejected the just-war theory as grounds for selective CO. See Griggs, "Selective CO," pp. 103–04; Baskir and Strauss, *Chance and Circumstance,* pp. 94–5.

49. Quote in Lewis I. Maddocks, "Legal and Constitutional Issues Regarding Conscientious Objectors," in June A. Willenz, ed., *Dialogue on the Draft* (Wash.: Am. Vets. Com., 1967), pp. 40–41; Judy Barrett, "The CO," working paper, National Advisory Commission on Selective Service (NACSS), Box 56, RG 220, N.A.; Alfred G. Killilea, "Privileging Conscientious Dissent: Another Look at Sherbert v. Verner", *Journal of Church and State* (1974), 16: p. 197n.

50. Sherk, "Position," p. 21; S.S. Case Law File, VF, 8 March 1965, LBH. In March, 1966, Hershey even expressed sympathy for those who had conscientious objection only to the Vietnam war. See Flynn, *Hershey,* p. 240; Lewis I. Maddocks, "Legal Aspects of CO," research paper, Paper, n.d., NACSS, Box 42, RG 220, N.A.

51. Quote in minutes of NACSS, 19 December 1966, p. 348, Box 90, RG 220; Brewster to Burke, 3 January 1967, Box 6, NACSS, ibid.; Rice, "Conscientious Objection," p. 75; Riga, "Selective," p. 162; Griggs, "Selective CO," p. 94. Although the theory of a just war had received no recognition in an official pronouncement by the church, it had achieved unofficial status through the writings of Augustine, Aquinas, and Suarez. Under rules developed by the famous Dutch jurist of the 17th century, Hugo Grotius, the principles for determining a just war were laid out: the decision for war had to be made by legitimate authority; the object was to vindicate justice; the war had to be waged with a just intent and under the control of a loving disposition and by just conduct; the damage inflicted had to be guided by the norm of proportionality; the war had to be the last resort.

52. NACSS, Record of Action, 7th meeting, 18–19 December 1966, Box 88, RG 220. National Advisory Commission on Selective Service, *In Pursuit of Equity: Who Serves When Not All Serve?* (Washington: USGPO, 1967), pp. 3-10; Flynn, *Hershey,* p. 242-48.

53. Gallup Poll 3: 2063; Flynn, *Hershey,* 235.

54. Gerhardt, *Draft,* pp. 300, 334–36; Reynolds to President, 22 June 1967, WHCF ND 9–4, Ct. 151, Lyndon B. Johnson Papers, Johnson Library, Austin, Texas (hereafter cited as LBJ); Rice, "Conscientious Objection," p. 73; *Statutes at Large,* 30 June 1967, 81 Stat. 104.

55. S.S., Annual Analysis of CO Work Program, VF 345.x5, 29 December 1967, LBH. The courts, however, was not so easily intimidated. In *United States v. Levy*, 419 F.2d 360 (8th Cir. 1969), the court held that eliminating the reference to "Supreme Being" and retaining "religous training and belief" worked no change in CO requirements which were still to be guided by the *Seeger* case.

56. Hershey interview, 15 December 1970, LBJ; S.S., September 1968, p. 3; *S.S.*, October 1968, p. 1; Omer to Levinson, 29 June 1967, WHCF ND 9-4, Ct. 153, LBJ; James W. Davis and Kenneth M. Dolbeare, "A Social Profile of Local Draft Board Members: the Case of Wisconsin," in Roger Little, ed., *Selective Service and American Society* (N.Y.: Russell Sage, 1969), p. 73; Baskir and Strauss, *Chance and Circumstance*, pp. 26, 40; Sherk, "Position," p. 22. Only four questions were asked on the new form. They dealt with the nature of the registrant's belief, how, where, and from what source he obtained his religious training and belief; the degree to which his beliefs would restrict his ability to serve as a noncombatant; and whether he had given public expression to his views. The personal appearance centered around the answers to these questions. All references to a "Supreme Being" were eliminated from forms.

57. S.S., *Semi-annual Report of the Director of Selective Service, January–June, 1973* (Wash.: USGPO, 1973), p. 55; Useem, *Conscription*, pp. 130-131; Baskir and Strauss, *Chance and Circumstance*, p. 41, cite a total of 172,000 during the "Vietnam Era," but do not indicate a source. Some critics argued that many CO's were railroaded into the army by local boards, but only a total of 17,000 servicemen made CO claims during the entire period. See Baskir and Strauss, *Chance and Circumstance*, p. 57.

58. Baskir and Strauss, *Chance and Circumstance*, pp. 41, 280-n.10, write that by late 1969, control atrophied and eventually 50,000 just dropped out without alternate service; Annual Analysis of CO Work Program, 29 December 1967, VF 345.x5; Sherk, "Position," p. 22; S.S., *Semi-annual Report of the Director of Selective Service, January 1–June 30, 1973* (Wash.: USGPO, 1973), p. 55. At the end of 1967, Selective Service conducted a comprehensive analysis of the alternate work program. Trends established in the 1950s had continued. The Mennonites continued to furnish the largest number by religious denomination, having well over 50 percent of all at work. From July 1952 to September 1967, they totaled 11,576, compared to only 661 for the Society of Friends, and 1,910 for the Church of the Brethren. No other religious group had over 1,000. Typical jobs remained the same, with most working in religious, private, and state hospitals both in the U.S. and abroad. Most of the jobs were arranged through the cooperation of peace churches. By 1968, more than fifty religious bodies were supporting the program. See Annual Analysis of CO Work Program, 29 December 1967, VF 345.x5, LBH; *S.S.*, March, 1966, p. 3; Sherk, "Position," p. 18. The typical CO was well educated with 42 percent being college graduates. See Peter Karsten, *Soldiers and Society: The Effects of Military Service and War on American Life* (Westport: Greenwood, 1978) p. 83.

59. S.S., *Semi-annual Report of the Director of Selective Service, January 1–June 30, 1970* (Wash.: USGPO, 1970), pp. 39-40.

60. S.S., *Semi-annual Report of the Director of Selective Service, July 1–December 31, 1970* (Wash.: USGPO, 1971) p. 8. Most local board members believed the courts were abetting draft dodging. But the courts had upheld the legality of the alternate service program. *O'Connor v. United States*, 415 F.2d 1110 (9th Cir., 1969). The system of extending liability because of poor job performance, however, did not meet approval: *United States v. Cook*,

abetting draft dodging. But the courts had upheld the legality of the alternate service program. *O'Connor v. United States*, 415 F.2d 1110 (9th Cir., 1969). The system of extending liability because of poor job performance, however, did not meet approval: *United States v. Cook*, 445 F.2d 883 (8th Cir., 1971). As for those CO's who refused to accept alternate work, prosecutions continued. From 1965 about 22,500 men were indicted for draft law violations and 8,756 were convicted, but only 4,001 were imprisoned. One study estimates that only a minority of the convictions involved conscientious or religious objection, and most of these were Jehovah's Witnesses. Although the law provided clear guidelines on violations, by 1970 lawyers were interjecting the entire question of the war before juries and obtaining acquittals. The uneven nature of enforcement contributed to Nixon's decision to end the draft. Baskir and Strauss, *Chance and Circumstance,* chap. III, p. 90ff, provide the figures. See also Kohn, *Jailed,* p. 87, 92; Brotsky, "Trail," pp. 103, 105, 109. See S.S., *Semi-annual Report, January 1–June 30, 1971,* p. 58 for CO summary report. In late 1970 and the first half of 1971, local boards handled an average of some 7,075 CO claims monthly for eight months. The total number of individuals who made such a claim totaled 76,486 and averaged 9,560 a month. The monthly average of those who were denied such a classification and then refused inductions was only 258.

61. James B. Jacobs & D. McNamara, "Selective Service Without a Draft," *Armed Forces and Society* (1984), 4: 368.

62. Wilson, "Evolution," p. 15.

63. Currently, West Germany's draft law allows a CO to be excused by a simple declaration. The Scandinavian nations also provide for simple application, but in Sweden some additional testimony is needed. France offered no CO classification until late 1963, but after the Algerian war, a system of alternate service emerged. In 1968, only 54 men out of 270,000 were classified as CO's. Great Britain ended the draft in the 1950s, but her CO system was the most tolerant, given comparable institutions and international responsibility. Churchill stated in March 1941, that persecution of such people "is odious to the British people." Both pacifists and political grounds were accepted. Local tribunals deliberated on such claims. The local tribunal could reject the application, or offer total exemption, or alternate service. Noncombat duty was also an option. The major difference with the U.S. system during World War II was the British option of a total exemption for a CO. During the war, about 86 men out of every 10,000 registered males applied for CO status. For Europe see Terrence Cullinan, "Models of Service Systems Overseas," in Friedman and Leistner, *Compulsory Service Systems,* p. 262; Albert A. Blum, "Comparative Conscription Systems: An Exploratory Analysis," in Little, *Survey,* pp. 458–59. For the British see "Memo on British CO's," n.d., VF 345.84H39, LBH; Griggs, "Selective CO's," p. 105; Peter Brock, *Twentieth Century Pacifism* (N.Y.: Van Nostrand, 1970), p. 158; Angus Calder, *The People's War: Britain, 1939–45* (N.Y.: Random House, 1969), p. 52; Arthur Marwick, *The Home Front: The British and the Second World War* (London: Thames & Hudson, 1976), p. 124.

4

A Pacifist's View
of Conscientious Objection

Gordon C. Zahn

In discussing any potentially controversial subject it is always best to make one's perspective and focus clear. I approach the subject from a combination of pacifist commitment and personal experience as a conscientious objector in the Civilian Public Service program during World War II. Either, perhaps, would be qualification enough; together, I would hope, they will provide additional depth and insights.

It is important to note that mine was, and is, not a "selective conscientious objection." However, the Center on Conscience and War, which I represent, endorses the Catholic bishops' repeated calls for changes in the law to provide for selective conscientious objection and see that simply as a matter of respecting individual rights that are now denied; second, even though we do not base our stand on the Catholic Church's traditional teachings, which distinguish between "just" and "unjust" war, we regard that denial as a form of religious discrimination against our fellow communicants who do adhere to those teachings—discrimination, needless to add, suffered as well by members of the other faiths and denominations which also accept that distinction.

The discrimination I encountered when I sought classification as a World War II CO took a different but obviously related form. Even though I was opposed to all war as the law required, my local board based its rejection of my claim on the assumption that, since the Catholic Church did not profess doctrinal pacifism, Catholics were not eligible for the CO classification. The recent re-discovery by my Church of the legitimacy of the pacifist position should spare Catholics of my persuasion similar difficulty in the event of a future draft, but it should not give them favored status over fellow-communicants who accept what is generally considered (mistaken though the judgment may be) the more orthodox Catholic interpretation of Christian responsibilities concerning war and military service.

Some might argue that the focus of this book is too narrow. If so, the fault lies in the nature of the Selective Service System and the law under which it operates. We begin with a crucial difference in definition, indeed a matter of principle. Recognition of conscientious objection is too often viewed as a privilege to be granted or withheld at the discretion of political or military authority—or even, as General Hershey dismissed it, an "indulgence extended to a few"—and not, as I would insist, a right. Simple logic, if not yet constitutional law, should make it clear that to impose any obligation requiring the citizen to act in a manner he or she sincerely judges to be immoral violates the spirit (and possibly the letter) of the First Amendment and, by so doing, is a betrayal of this nation's professed commitment to religious freedom.

After all, we are not dealing with one of those troubling situations where the public authority feels compelled to restrain or forbid religious practices it considers injurious to the common good (ritual cannibalism, to suggest an extreme example). Denying the legitimate conscientious objector exemption from active participation in war or training for war would be enforced compliance, under threat of punitive sanction, with actions contrary to his religious commitment and moral obligations. That is an altogether different matter.

It is the failure to recognize this that has accounted for much of the difficulty encountered in the past. The law (and Selective Service as its instrument) should have no function other than to establish that a refusal to accept induction is religious in nature and sincerely held. Indeed even that may be allowing too much: given the legitimate pride we take in a jurisprudence based on the presumption of innocence, I would suggest that the prospective CO ought to be presumed sincere until proven otherwise. Be that as it may, the law as now applied and administered, by seeking to specify acceptable terms and content for religious conscientious objection actually promotes preferential treatment of one religious belief system, the so-called "peace church" model, over others.

My best contribution, I believe, is to assess the history of the relationship between Selective Service and the Conscientious Objector from that perspective of one who has experienced that relationship "from the inside," so to speak.

I am inclined to put greater weight than Professor Flynn does on the fact that Selective Service, as we have known it for more than forty years, began as peacetime conscription. I incline toward the opinion that this probably explains why any provision for formal recognition of conscientious objection was made in the first place. Once war came and an alternative service program was introduced, the intent, as Professor Flynn shows, was laudable enough: it was to the advantage of the peace community and the Selective Service bureaucracy that matters be handled as smoothly as possible so that any repetition of the maltreatment to which objectors in World War I had been exposed might be avoided. Civilian Public Service (CPS), it was hoped, would constitute recognition of sincerely held religious objections to war and military service and, at the same time, provide the opportunity to perform truly meaningful non-military service to the nation.

It would be too much to say the effort failed completely, but those who would hail it as a successful demonstration of democratic ideals in practice fall even wider of the mark. Though the World War I extremes of physical brutality were not repeated, CPS did incorporate a significant measure of psychological duress and penalty. The denial of compensation for work performed or any of the benefits extended to men in the other services was a thinly veiled price placed upon the exercise of conscience. Similarly, though one can justify requiring that objectors not be assigned to service in or near their home communities, the actual choice of remote and isolated camp locations may have been due in greater part to General Hershey's expressed conviction that "the conscientious objector is handled best if no one hears of him."

More serious in their implications were actions and policies designed to limit or interfere with the assignees' exercise of civil rights (always undertaken in the interests of avoiding "bad public relations," of course). Thus, in 1942 a Selective Service official, in the course of an inspection visit to the Alexian Brothers' Hospital CPS unit in Chicago, was asked, "The supreme law of the land is Selective Service then, and not the Constitution?" To which the official replied, "At the present time it is."

General Hershey probably would have been more circumspect in his response, but the exchange does reflect an inherent lack of sensitivity in Selective Service policy and action. If in public rhetoric and private conversations with leaders of the pacifist community, General Hershey, Col. Kosch, and other Selective Service officials repeatedly affirmed the virtues of fairness and equity in the treatment of conscientious objectors (as long as they were willing to behave themselves and avoid public controversy), this must be weighed against the obvious and often shocking inequities in actual Selective Service practice. Men were routinely inducted into Civilian Public Service who never would have been accepted by the military. Once in, it was not easy to get out.

As Professor Flynn notes there were frequent complaints from men in the Program that the administration of what was billed as "work of national importance under civilian direction" failed on both counts. Most of the work projects fell far short of the promise, and his direction was placed in the hands of men whose careers and commitment were military in orientation and who, predictably enough, had little understanding of—or respect for—men who rejected the military and its values.

To give him his due, General Hershey did try to protect CPS from the more vindictive attacks and demands of Congressmen, veterans organizations, jingo-journalists, and the like. The protection, however, took the form of cushioning and compromising—in almost every case at the expense of those he was protecting. Indeed, there are perfectly good sociological reasons to assume that he and the officials around him shared the general disapproval of conscientious objectors. Given the circumstances, it is likely that concern for bureaucratic convenience and defence of "turf" may offer a better explanation for those efforts to forestall adverse public reaction than concern for the men themselves or respect for their rights.

Truly meaningful non-military service opportunities were only occasionally (and then reluctantly) made available to the men in camp. For one thing, such assignments freed the CPS workers from the isolation of the camps (although it was made clear enough that any "misbehavior" made them subject to quick return) and removed them from the more direct control of Selective Service headquarters. In my study of the Warner camp to which I was assigned,[1] I made two admittedly severe judgments which I see no reason to change. As I see it, the CPS program is best described as "work of national unimportance under military direction" and, whether so intended or not, represented an experiment in the democratic suppression of a dissident minority in time of war.

Today discussion of Selective Service and the conscientious objector takes place in a different and far more congenial atmosphere. This means that whatever changes are necessary, if we are to avoid the shortcomings of the past, must be made now. Once a draft is in operation or the nation is again involved in active hostilities, the pressure will all be in the opposite direction. The essential first step is to revise the law so that the conscientious objector classification will be broadened to make it available to anyone who can establish a valid religious opposition to any or every war in which he (or she) is likely to be ordered to take part.

But that is only a first step in the much needed redefinition of the relationship between Selective Service and the conscientious objector. Once that goal is achieved, steps should be taken to assure that the determination of the legitimacy and sincerity of an applicant's religious objection is not left to the militarily-oriented officials of the Selective Service System or to local boards charged with responsibility for producing recruits for the armed forces. While I do not delude myself into believing that academics, churchmen, and the like are immune to war-hysteria, an independent review body composed of such persons could offer greater hope of objectivity.

Once the decision is reached, and the conscientious objectors assigned to alternate service, the Selective Service System should have no further responsibility for, or authority over, them. Just as the individuals assigned to military service are immediately released to the jurisdiction of the various armed forces, so should the alternate service inductee be released to the employing agency which would thereafter bear full responsibility for supervising and evaluating the adequacy of his performance.

In summary, I would suggest that the relationship between Selective Service and the Conscientious Objector is handled best if they have as little as possible to do with each other. Professor Flynn is correct in his assessment of the improved situation since World War II, but this should be seen in the context of current Selective Service planning which hints at a reversion to the less than satisfactory attitudes and practices of the past. I second his endorsement of a proposal which would allow a man to declare himself a CO and be dropped from the rolls but not simply, or even primarily, as a concession to bureaucratic convenience and efficiency. The issue we address is more than a matter of numbers, totals, and percentages. In a very real sense recognition of selective conscientious objection is a test of our commitment to the values of religious freedom we profess to cherish and, it follows from that, a measure of our national integrity.

Notes

1.   Gordon Zahn, *Another Part of the War: The Camp Simon Story* (Amherst: U. of Mass., 1979).

5

The U.S. Catholic Bishops and Selective Conscientious Objection: History and Logic of the Position

J. Bryan Hehir

The purpose of this chapter is to trace the history and content of the U.S. Catholic bishops' position on Selective Conscientious Objection (SCO). The paper will proceed in three steps: (1) an interpretation of the development and logic of Catholic moral teaching on warfare; (2) an exposition of the specific statements on SCO made by the bishops; and (3) a commentary on the questions which flow from the tradition and the position of SCO.

Catholic Teaching on War and Peace: A Synthetic Statement

The U.S. bishops' statements on SCO cover a period from 1971 to 1983. To set the conceptual background for these statements I will trace the main lines of Catholic thinking on war and peace through the issuance of the pastoral letter, *The Challenge of Peace: God's Promise and Our Response* in May 1983.

The Classical Legacy: Its Development

Historical surveys of Christian teaching on war conventionally employ Roland H. Bainton's *Christian Attitudes Toward War and Peace* as a convenient, if not definitive, classification of positions.[1] Bainton portrays a direct and continuing relationship between the just-war doctrine and the Catholic church. The relationship is historical rather than doctrinal; the just-war ethic is not exclusively a Christian preserve but it has been most extensively cultivated within the Roman Catholic moral tradition.

LeRoy B. Walters concludes his illuminating study of five just-war authors with the observation that there exist several just-war theories within a single just-war tradition.[2] While acknowledging this doctrinal pluralism, the focus in this section is to specify the relationship between the just-war tradition and the Catholic tradition. This relationship can be illustrated with new clarity and precision today thanks to a series of excellent historical studies on just-war theories which have appeared in the last decade.[3] On the basis of these studies it is possible to distinguish four stages of development of just-war thought in the Catholic tradition. The four stages are associated with distinctive personalities: Augustine (d. 430), Aquinas (d. 1274), the Spanish Scholastics (Vitoria, d. 1546, and Suarez, d. 1617), and twentieth-century papal teaching. In the context of this article it is possible only to identify the broad lines of development within the just-war tradition and to summarize the conceptual product of just-war norms as they exist today.

Augustine provided the basic rationale for other just-war theorists, by utilizing a moral argument which legitimized the use of force as a means of implementing the Gospel command of love in the political order.[4] Augustine's argument is political in the sense that his moral judgment on warfare emerged from an assessment of the possibilities and requirements of order in the political community. Augustine's theological anthropology is marked by an abiding consciousness of the effect of sin in human affairs. War is both the product of sin and a remedy for it; in a world marked by sin, the use of force by public authorities is a legitimate means of avenging evil. In the face of the New Testament ethic, most powerfully evident in the Sermon on the Mount, the use of force was problematical for Christians but not impossible to reconcile with the Gospel. Augustine combined an ethic of intention with a powerful sense of the needs of public order in constructing a position which prohibited killing in self-defense, but acknowledged its possibility in social relations.[5]

Thomas Aquinas inherited the Augustinian position, accepted its basic rationale, and provided the just-war theory with a systematic set of criteria: just-cause, legitimate authority and right intention.[6] Following Augustine, Thomas located his analysis of just-war within the framework of an ethic of charity and tied it directly to the needs of the common good. The taking of human life remained a major moral problem for those committed to the message and life of Jesus; it could be justified only be referring it to the defense of the common good. The purpose of the just-war ethic was not to rationalize violence, but to limit its scope and methods in a world where force was a tragic but necessary instrument of the political process.

The ambivalence of legitimizing even a limited use of force within an evangelical ethic appears in Thomas' discussion of the right of self-defense. Augustine had prohibited the killing of another in the name of self-defense. Aquinas accepted the measure, but only by using the principle of double effect: public authorities could directly will the taking of life, but private persons could *intend* only the deterring of aggression, not the death of the aggressor.[7] The principal role of Aquinas in the just-war tradition was that he systematized the limiting criteria which had developed since Augustine, and he added his immense authority in Catholic theological tradition to the just-war concept.

Aquinas did theology in the context of a unified Christian commonwealth with the church established as the recognized moral authority. By the time Vitoria and Suarez addressed the problem of war two decisive changes had occurred. First, the emergence of the nation-state produced a qualitatively new center of secular political authority which challenged both the idea of a wider Christian common-wealth and the binding power of any universal moral authority higher than the state. Second, the impact of the Reformation eroded the spiritual and moral bonds of the Christian community which Augustine and Aquinas had taken for granted. Faced with a new political and religious context, the Spanish Scholastics labored to save the substance of the just-war ethic by revising its structure.[8] The emphasis of the normative teaching shifted from Aquinas' strong stress on just-cause toward a concentration on questions of means used in warfare. The category of just-cause war was modified to allow for the possibility that both sides subjectively perceived themselves to have justifiable reasons for war. In the face of this principle, itself an accommodation to the secular nation-state, the moralists made a tactical retreat to the position of seeking to limit the scope of violence among states. In recasting the content of the just-cause category and in enhancing the status of judgments about the means of warfare, the Spanish Scholastics, and to an even greater degree the Protestant theologian Hugo Grotius (d. 1645), provided the foundation for the secular science of international law.[9]

Between the seventeenth and twentieth centuries the only innovative contribution to just-war thinking in the Catholic tradition was the work of Taparelli d'Azeglio (d. 1862) in the nineteenth century. His efforts to think about the international community as a subject of moral law provided the conceptual foundation for themes in twentieth century papal teaching. For the purposes of this survey, it is more useful to examine the product of the papal teaching rather than its roots. The principal link in the relationship of the just-war tradition and papal teaching is Pius XII (d. 1958). In a detailed analysis of Pius XII's teaching on modern warfare, John Courtney Murray illustrates how Pius XII both affirmed the just-war ethic and modified its content.[10]

On the one hand, Pius XII's approach to war acknowledged the possibility that force could be used as an instrument of justice, although he consistently tried to place this question within the framework of the need for creating a more adequate political and legal structure for the international community.[11] On the other hand, Pius XII was sufficiently impressed, on both moral and political grounds, with the destructive capacity of modern warfare that he reduced the legitimate causes of war from three (defense, avenging evil, and restoring violated rights) to one:

defense of one's nation or of others being unjustly attacked.[12] This marginal justification of the legitimacy of force in international relations foreshadowed the increasing discomfort which papal teaching would have reconciling modern weaponry with standards of reason and faith. At the same time Pius XII was vividly clear that pacifism as moral posture was unacceptable. This included a judgment that conscientious objection also was unacceptable.[13]

Conciliar and Post-Conciliar Teaching: Its Direction

In the thirty years since John XXIII took up the papal ministry, Catholic teaching on war has been in a state of movement. The principal development has been the legitimation for individuals of a pacifist perspective as a method for evaluating modern warfare. This has occurred as one piece of a larger pattern, so the pacifist orientation in contemporary teaching should not be seen as an isolated phenomenon. The task here is to assess both its meaning and its status in relationship to just-war thinking within Catholicism. The relevant texts which have produced the pacifist option are John XXIII's *Pacem In Terris* (1963); Vatican II's *Gaudium et Spes* (1965) and a series of statements by Paul VI during his pontificate (1963–1978).[14]

Both *Pacem In Terris* and *Gaudium et Spes* have contributed to the articulation of a pacifist position within Catholicism, but they have done so in different ways. The analysis of modern war in *Pacem In Terris* is notable for three reasons. First, the strong criticism of the arms race, and the balance of terror upon which it rests, is linked directly to positive proposals much like those of Pius XII, calling for structural reform of the international political and legal system. In Pope John's view the control of the arms race is one of several questions which exhibit the structural defect in international relations today. Second, *Pacem In Terris,* alone in the documents of contemporary papal teaching, provides no explicit endorsement of the right of self-defense for peoples and states. Third, the most explicit moral judgment asserted in the section on war seems to call into question the very rationale of just-war teaching. The rendition of the text has itself been the subject of extensive controversy. The most widely used version asserts: "Therefore, in this age of ours, which prides itself on its atomic power, it is irrational to think that war is a proper way to obtain justice for violated rights."[15]

Some commentators, like James Douglass, have read this statement to mean that the conditions of modern war are such that no form of warfare can be justified.[16] The passage is, therefore, a pure pacifist assertion. Others, like Paul Ramsey, contend that such an interpretation cannot be sustained. Ramsey sees *Pacem In Terris* simply reaffirming the position of Pius XII: that defensive war is the only permissible recourse to force in the nuclear age.[17] This dispute over the "literal sense" of *Pacem In Terris* remains unresolved and may be not open to definitive resolution. In the face of contending views, the approach taken here is to place *Pacem In Terris* in the line of what preceded it and followed it in papal teaching. Since later documents consistently assert the right of legitimate defense for states, and yet make no attempt to reform, correct or reinterpret *Pacem In Terris,* it seems reasonable to assume that the encyclical is not understood in Catholic teaching as proscribing the defensive use of force under very restricted conditions. Even if this reading of the text is accepted, it amounts to toleration of the use of force not a moral endorsement. Both the tenor and the text of *Pacem In Terris* signaled a changing atmosphere in the Catholic evaluation of modern war.

In spite of his devastating critique of war, John XXIII provided no explicit endorsement of a pacifist position. This occurred for the first time in Catholic teaching in *Gaudium et Spes.* The tone of this conciliar reflection on war and peace is set by its expressed intention "to undertake an evaluation of war with an entirely new attitude." Two products of this new attitude are the endorsement of nonviolent philosophy and support for conscientious objection. The first occurs in the context of the conciliar reflection on the nature and meaning of peace: "we cannot fail to praise those who renounce the use of violence in the vindication of their rights, and who resort to methods of defense which are otherwise available to weaker parties too, provided that this can be done without injury to the rights and duties of others or of the community itself."[18] From the perspective of ethical analysis, an endorsement *in principle* of a nonviolent position would have been conceptually more clear. As the text stands in *Gaudium et Spes,* it is closer to being a pastoral commendation of those practicing nonviolence than it is a statement of moral principle. In spite of this ambiguity, it does not distort the text to find in this passage support for a pacifist position as a legitimate option for the Catholic conscience.

Such an interpretation is confirmed in the next paragraph by the discussion in *Gaudium et Spes* of the obligation of conscience in the face of policy directives. In language noticeably stronger than earlier authors had used, the Council calls upon Christians to resist orders which violate the natural law. In this context *Gaudium et Spes* addresses conscientious objection: "It seems right that laws make humane provisions for the case of those who for reasons of conscience refuse to bear arms, provided however, that they accept some other form of service to the human community."[19]

No distinction is made here between universal and selective conscientious objection. While this omission leaves some issues unresolved, the thrust of the statement as it stands makes clear that in supporting universal conscientious objection, the Council has placed the church in support of those individuals who affirm a clear-cut pacifist position.

Both statements in *Gaudium et Spes* are strikingly different from a just-war position, and the statement on conscientious objection reversed the position taken by Pius XII a decade earlier. In the years after the Council, Paul VI contributed to the direction taken in these statements by praising nonviolent methods of social change.[20] Taken together, a series of statements from *Pacem In Terris* through the speeches of Paul VI have established a new position from which Catholics can evaluate the moral problem of war. The question which inevitably arises in light of these statements is whether Catholic teaching has simply become pacifist. Such an impression can be garnered from some of the commentaries on recent church teaching. James Douglass' position that *Pacem In Terris* is a pacifist document has already been cited.[21] John Yoder, in his work, *Nevertheless: The Varieties of Religious Pacifism* classifies *Pacem In Terris* and Pope Paul's *Address to the United Nations* (1965) as examples of cosmopolitan pacifism.[22] In a statement submitted to the U.N. Special Session on Disarmament (1978), Pax Christi, an International Catholic Movement for Peace, made the following judgment about the state of mind of Catholics: "Concerned Catholics, in finding the traditional conditions for organizing violence inapplicable are concentrating on the theology of peace, a theology based on the centrality of love and on seeing the imprint of the divine in every human creature."[23]

The difficulty with these statements is that they push the texts too far. The total content of recent Catholic teaching does not support a judgment that the church has moved from a just-war ethic to a pacifist position. The reality is both more complex, less clear, and perhaps, morally richer than such an absolute "conversion" would be. There has been a dimension of change in the normative doctrine on war; its significance can be evaluated from the texts examined above, and from others which support and compliment these. But there has also been affirmed a significant line of continuity with the teaching of Pius XII, and with the moral tradition of the just-war ethic.

The central theme which ties contemporary Catholic teaching to earlier just-war teaching is the repeated assertion of the right of states to legitimate defense. The relevant texts, in addition to Pius XII, are *Gaudium et Spes*, Pope Paul's U.N. Address and the Vatican Statement, *The Holy See and Disarmament at the U.N.* (1976).[24] The substance of these assertions is basically the same: in a world of states, still devoid of an effective political-legal international authority, "governments cannot be denied the right to legitimate defense once every means of peaceful settlement has been exhausted."[25] Implied in this statement, and others like it, is a structure of moral argument which we have already examined.

The term "just-war" does not appear in recent papal teaching, but if the right of legitimate defense is affirmed, then just below the surface of the affirmation lies what Ralph B. Potter has called the "moral logic" of just-war theory. This moral logic is the set of questions used to determine when recourse to arms is a "legitimate" act of defense and when it is not. To assert the right of states to defend themselves without providing a moral framework for the assertion is to leave the road open to indiscriminate uses of force. The assertion requires an ethical calculus defining both the legitimate ends and limited means which keep the use of force within the moral universe.

In fact *Gaudium et Spes* uses the traditional ethical calculus but does not identify it as such. The categories which legitimate some forms of force and prohibit others invoke terms like "just defense," rely upon the principle of proportionality, and use the rule of noncombatant immunity as the key concept in the Council's condemnation of weapons of mass destruction. The prominent use of the traditional categories illustrates that, even in the document which formulated a pacifist option, Catholic moral theology retained the conviction that war is possible, may be necessary in the name of justice, and, if necessary, must be a rule-governed activity pursued within a fabric of moral restraints.

The use of the traditional ethical calculus is also reflected in the way the arms race is treated in recent Catholic teaching. At one level the statements, from *Pacem In Terris* through *Gaudium et Spes* to the *Holy See and Disarmament*, are a relentless condemnation of the arms race. The passage from *Gaudium et Spes* is representative: "the arms race is an utterly treacherous trap for humanity, and one which injures the poor to an intolerable degree."[26] The judgment is reiterated with qualitatively new strength a decade after Vatican II. In an intervention at the United Nations, the Holy See urged that the arms race "be condemned unreservedly" because it is "a danger, an injustice, a theft from the poor and a folly."[27] Given the dimensions and danger of the nuclear arms race, the power of these statements establishes for the Holy See a position which is morally prophetic and politically important.

Equally significant, however, is the difference in tone and style in the papal discourse when it moves from condemnation of the arms race to constructive political change. The approach to arms control and disarmament is cautious and carefully drawn. It reflects awareness of the complexity of negotiating an agreement between sovereign states on an issue central to their security. The passage which typifies the recent teaching on disarmament is found in *Gaudium et Spes:* "Hence everyone must labor to put an end at last to the arms race, and to make a true beginning of disarmament, not indeed a unilateral disarmament, but one proceeding at an equal pace according to agreement, and backed up by authentic and workable safeguards."[28]

The statements in Catholic teaching call for a fundamental change in the psychology and politics of interstate relations, from fear to mutual trust; understandably, they provide little guidance about which specific policy measures should be pursued to control the arms race. They do, however, offer a set of procedural criteria which reflect the approach just cited from *Gaudium et Spes*. The process of disarmament must be "gradual," "controlled," and "backed up by genuine and effective guarantees."[29] These operational guidelines are the product of a measured political realism in the face of a situation which urgently requires transformation, but which does not yield to simple solutions. The papal appeals for disarmament carefully try to incorporate both dimensions of the dilemma, prophetic vision and political wisdom.[30] John Paul II in his own distinctive fashion blends both of these themes.

John Paul II

John Paul II has identified the pursuit of peace within nations and among nations as a major objective of his pontificate. In pursuit of this goal the Pope teaches, travels and takes specific initiatives to prevent resort to force as a method of solving conflicts.

The content of John Paul's teaching on war and peace reflects the main themes of the post-conciliar period. He was a major influence in the shaping of *Gaudium et Spes* at Vatican II, and his pontifical statements combine an appeal for non-violent solutions with a recognition that the state of world politics continues to legitimate the right of self-defense on the part of nations and peoples.

Some addresses, particularly those aimed at conflict within nations, stress exclusively "the nonviolent option"; the classical example was the Pope's speech at Drogheda, Ireland. In making a dramatic plea to all actors in the Irish tragedy he pressed his case to the point where he seemed to threaten the classical affirmation that force could, in some instances, be a remedy for injustice. No such claim is found at Drogheda. Instead the theme of the address was captured in the following words:

> I join my voice today to the voice of Paul VI and my other predecessors, to the voices of your religious leaders, to the voices of all men and women of reason, and I proclaim with the conviction of my faith in Christ and with an awareness of my mission, that violence is evil, that violence is unacceptable as a solution to problems, that violence is unworthy of man. Violence destroys what it claims to defend: the dignity, the life, the freedom of human beings.[31]

It can be argued, from the context of the speech and the linking of "violence" with "murder" later in this paragraph that the Pope in fact was using a classical distinction to contrast "violence" (indiscriminate force) with force (measured use of power), but no explicit differentiation is made. I use the text because there are others like it, where the Pope's words do not fit the standard just-war logic or language.

There are other texts, however, where the line of continuity with Augustine and Aquinas is made clear. The most specific is the 1982 *World Day of Peace Message*. The argument is Augustinian in its movement from theological anthropology to political analysis and an ethic of legitimate defense. The Pope grounds his argument in anthropology: "In the final analysis, when we consider the question of peace, we are led to consider the meaning and conditions of our own personal and community lives."[32] He then makes his political assessment: "For Christians know that in this world a totally and permanently peaceful human society is unfortunately a utopia, and that ideologies that hold up that prospect as easily attainable are based on hopes that cannot be realized, whatever the reason behind them."[33] In light of this assessment, John Paul II then affirms the classical tradition: "That is why Christians. . .have no hesitation in recalling that, in the name of an elementary requirement of justice, peoples have a right and even a duty to protect their existence and freedom by proportionate means against an unjust aggressor (cf. Guadium et Spes, 79)."[34]

In other contexts the Pope has reiterated this theme even as he continues to press political solutions for both internal and international conflicts.

The Challenge of Peace

The 1983 pastoral letter is one of the texts where the U.S. Bishops' position on SCO is stated, but my concern in this section is simply to relate the moral theory of the letter to the interpretation offered here of the wider Catholic tradition. The fundamental structure of *The Challenge of Peace* is a just-war ethic used to analyze the nuclear age. The policy chapter on force (Chapter 2) employs the means criteria of just-war theory to evaluate both the use of nuclear weapons and the strategy of deterrence. In both the policy section and the pastoral section (Chapter 5) norms for conscience formation based on just-war premises are prominent.

At the level of personal choice, a clear option is made available to those who "renounce the use of violence in the vindication of their rights." The personal possibility—designated as such in the letter—is based on the section of the pastoral entitled "The Value of Non-Violence." This moral argument, of course, is not directly pertinent to SCO but to conscientious objection to all war. The fact that such a choice is today legitimated for Catholics demonstrates a shift in the Church's teaching since 1956 when Pius XII ruled out such an option. The shift, however, was not from just-war to a totally new posture for Catholicism. While maintaining basic continuity with the ethic as its public policy position, Catholic teaching opened space for a personal option which had been absent in the official teaching for many centuries.

The U.S. Bishops on SCO: The Record

The framework of Catholic teaching on war and peace, as it developed after Vatican II, allowed for three distinct possibilities at the level of personal conscience: participation in a just-war; conscientious objection to all warfare; and selective conscientious objection based on just-war criteria. While this range of choices was contained in the framework of the moral theory, it was the catalytic effect of the Vietnam War which evoked the three distinct positions. The resurgence of the nuclear debate in the 1980s provided added impetus for the three options.

In the period from 1968 through 1983, the U.S. Bishops made four statements touching on SCO. These were: *Human Life in Our Day* (1968); *Declaration on Conscientious Objection and Selective Conscientious Objection* (1971); *Statement on Registration and Conscription for Military Service* (1980); and *The Challenge of Peace* (1983). I will discuss the role of these statements, then comment on the content of each.

Catholic teaching on war and peace has traditionally had two purposes: a *pastoral* function to aid in the formation of conscience for the individual; and a *policy* function to help set the right terms of public debate on war and peace in civil society. The teaching on SCO is primarily addressed to the pastoral level of individual decisionmaking, but it has significant policy consequences. When the U.S. Bishops developed their first two statements on SCO (1968 and 1971) the Vietnam War was at its peak and the bishops had not played a major role in the public policy debate. It was clear, however, at the pastoral level that the choices the war imposed on draft-age Catholics were creating havoc in their lives. Although the bishops never exercised a major influence on Vietnam policy, they channeled their energies in the direction of personal conscience formation with this series of statements.

Human Life in Our Day (1968)

The pastoral letter issued in 1968 had a primary and secondary objective. The primary purpose was to provide the U.S. Bishops with a vehicle to respond to the encyclical *Humanae Vitae* (1968) on Catholic teaching on contraception. In Part One of the pastoral the bishops sought to provide support to Paul VI's teaching and also to respond to the theological and pastoral turmoil which the encyclical had sparked in the United States.

The secondary purpose was to have the bishops comment on the war in Vietnam, an event creating even more turmoil in civil society than *Humanae Vitae* caused in the church. The bishops bridged the gap between these disparate questions (contraception and war) by stressing two themes: the defense of life and the pivotal role of personal conscience in moral decisionmaking.

The question of conscience, its relationship to the objective moral law and its role as the ultimate sanctuary where a person accepts responsibility for action has been a central theme in the contraception controversy. The bishops used the occasion to stress the theology of conscience, particularly in the light of increasingly complex moral questions touching the beginning of human life. This pastoral letter preceded the Supreme Court's decision on abortion (1973) and the range of proliferating technologies affecting conception and birth which are addressed in the recent Vatican *Instruction* (March 10, 1987), but it highlighted the conscience question for a "simpler" issue.

The bishops then extended the human life/conscience categories to the topic of modern warfare. Vietnam was not the focus of the analysis, only a part of it. On the Vietnam policy debate the bishops confined their comments to raising questions about the proportionality of the war. At the level of personal conscience they followed the logic of *Gaudium et Spes* in stressing the weighty burden which falls on personal conscience because of the nature of modern war. In the words of the conciliar text: "the council wishes, above all things else, to recall the permanent binding force of universal natural law and its all-embracing principles. Man's conscience itself gives ever more emphatic voice to these principles. Therefore, actions which deliberately conflict with these same principles, as well as orders commanding such actions are criminal, and blind obedience cannot excuse those who yield to them."[35]

The American pastoral letter pressed the statements of *Gaudium et Spes* to a specific conclusion. The conciliar text had not discussed SCO, but logic of its principles contained the foundation of an SCO position. The bishops cited the passages praising nonviolent measures and calling for civil law to make humane provision for conscientious objections. Then *Human Life In Our Day* stated:

> We therefore recommend a modification of the Selective Service Act, making it possible, although not easy, for so-called selective conscientious objectors to refuse— without fear of imprisonment or loss of citizenship—to serve in wars which they consider unjust or in branches of the service (e.g. the strategic nuclear forces) which would subject them to the performance of actions contrary to deeply held moral convictions about indiscriminate killing. Some other forms of service to the human community should be required of those so exempted.[36]

The pastoral letter did not go beyond this precise statement; it neither grounded the claim in the longer tradition of just-war, nor did it expand upon the difficulties of implementing this proposal.

Declaration on Conscientious Objection and Selective Conscientious Objection (1971)

The 1971 *Declaration* is the most expansive and explicit statement the bishops have made on SCO. Again they chose to ground their proposal in the teaching of the Second Vatican Council. The 1971 statement draws its general teaching on conscience from *Dignitatis Humanae* and *Gaudium et Spes*. It then reiterates the texts from *Gaudium et Spes* on conscience and objection to war, noting in a pointed reference that many in civil society are mistaken about Catholic teaching. The reference was to the difficulty some young Catholics were having to convince draft boards that Catholic teaching had moved beyond Pius XII on conscientious objection.[37]

The essential affirmation of the 1971 *Declaration* is the following text:

> In the light of the Gospel and from an analysis of the Church's teaching on conscience, it is clear that a Catholic can be a conscientious objector to war in general or to a particular war because of religious training and belief. . . . As we hold individuals in high esteem who conscientiously serve in the armed forces, so also we should regard conscientious objection and selective conscientious objection as positive indicators within the Church of a sound moral awareness and respect for human life.[37]

Whereas the Vatican Council's teaching about conscience and war had not distinguished between general and selective objection, the bishops' statement specified both and joined them in a single sweeping statement. The statement had already specified responsible participation in war as a valid conclusion of Catholic teaching on the common good.

The 1971 *Declaration* makes two steps beyond *Human Life In Our Day*. First, it acknowledges the procedural and practical difficulties of moving from the moral statement supporting SCO to policy and civil law. The *Declaration* calls "upon moralists, lawyers and civil servants to work cooperatively toward a policy which can reconcile the demands of the moral and civic order concerning this issue."[38] Second, again in response to a growing pastoral problem of the 1970s, the bishops address the case of those who have left the United States or been imprisoned rather than be drafted. The bishops call—as they would again in the later 1970s—for amnesty for imprisoned SCOs and for repatriation of those willing "to return to the country to show responsibility for their conduct"[39] and a willingness to serve the common good in alternative ways.

After the *Declaration* of 1971 no new content on SCO is added to the episcopal position, but a new issue was added in 1980.

Statement on Registration and Conscription
for Military Service (1980)

The Vietnam debate of the 1970s had resulted in the repeal of the system of military conscription. The United States had reverted to an all volunteer military force. In the late 1970s, the Carter Administration had moved to reinstitute registration for military service, but not to reinstate the system of conscription. While the U.S. Bishops had consistently opposed (since 1944) peacetime military conscription, they had never addressed the specific question of the state's right to call for registration alone.

The intensity of conviction and feeling which had been part of the Vietnam debate made any move toward registration suspect of being a foil for the second step of restoring universal military conscription. Precisely because the bishops had been more involved in the personal rather than the policy dimensions of the earlier debate, there was some interest in how they would address the registration question. The 1980 *Statement* began with a moral argument about the correlative rights and duties of civil authorities and citizens regarding the common defense. Essentially the argument was an affirmation of the state's duty to defend society, its right to call citizens to that effort and the limits which Catholic moral teaching put on the state's right to use force. Then the bishops affirmed the responsibilities which citizens had toward the common good, as well as the need to assess the call of the state to military service in a moral framework. The centrality of conscience in this dialogue of citizen and state was again stressed.

On the specific issue of registration, the bishops acknowledged the right of the state to register citizens, but they asked that reasons for the call be offered. In taking this position the bishops set themselves apart from some who were urging resistance to the registration in principle. On peacetime conscription and general conscientious objection, the bishops repeated their earlier positions.

On SCO, the 1980 *Statement* identified the SCO claim as "a moral conclusion which can be validly derived from the classical moral teaching of just-war theory."[40] This was the first time the episcopal conference reached back prior to Vatican II to the classical tradition of Vitoria and Suarez on SCO. Another first for the 1980 *Statement* was that it specified *jus ad bellum* as well as *jus in bello** reasons as a possible basis for SCO. This addition was significant because it moved the SCO reasoning beyond the Vietnam and nuclear war cases, both of which focused on means questions.

The *Statement* again acknowledged the difficulty of translating this morally valid claim into civil law—no progress on that had been made since 1971.

The Challenge of Peace (1983)

The pastoral letter of 1983, the first pastoral to address war and peace in any detail since *Human Life In Our Day*, simply reiterated the 1971 *Declaration* on SCO. The pastoral did not add any substantive elements to the earlier argument. What it did provide was a much more detailed assessment of the nuclear dilemma which opened possibilities for SCO claims regarding the use of nuclear weapons and the strategy of deterrence. The pastoral drew no such conclusions—save the absolute prohibition it placed on using weapons against civilian centers. Even the controversial "No First Use" section allowed for disagreement and dissent.

---

* Editor's Note: *Jus ad bellum* refers to rules for determining the legal validity of a war. *Jus in bello* relates to rules regarding the validity of actions taken in war.

Beyond the Bishops: The Unfinished Agenda

From 1968 to 1983 the U.S. bishops established a position on SCO in the public policy arena. It was rooted in the just-war ethic and it coexisted with a continuing moral legitimation of Catholics serving in the armed forces and with Catholics holding a position of conscientious objection. The position was a moral claim for SCO, not a finished policy proposal. The bishops recognized that they needed other voices and other competencies to move SCO from the moral order into law and policy. The bishops invited other professions and disciplines into the effort to shape an SCO position in American law. There remain four categories of issues where the statements of the last twenty-five years by popes, the Council and the episcopal conference require further development.

Theological Questions: A basic theological-ethical issue which requires more debate and analysis in the Catholic tradition is the way in which the just-war and pacifist arguments relate to each other. In an earlier essay I argued that the two traditions were distinct in modes of reasoning and led to diverse conclusions which could not be collapsed into a single judgment.[41] The just-war ethic leads to either responsible participation or SCO; the pacifist position leads to conscientious objection. I also argued, and still maintain, that the two positions share key value judgments (i.e., the sacredness of human life, the prohibition against attacking innocent life, the refusal to allow war to be assessed on purely "realist" grounds apart from moral reasoning). Moreover, I hold with Ralph B. Potter and James Childress that the moral reasoning of the just-war ethic begins with a presumption against the use of force and then provides for a series of exceptional cases where the presumption is overridden.[42] This presumption is a common point of origin for both just-war and pacifist reasoning but the road taken by each moves in different directions.

The *Challenge of Peace* went beyond my comparison of the two traditions on the basis of shared values and a common starting point to an argument that the traditions were complementary even through they led to different personal and policy conclusions.[43] James Finn has argued that pressing the two traditions toward a complementary posture corrupts both rather than strengthening either.[44] I am not convinced by Mr. Finn's argument, but I am sure the topic needs more analysis.

As the interpretation I have offered indicates, much of the movement toward a pacifist option in Catholicism is the product of the last twenty-five years. There is need to systematize the two strains of thinking which have emerged to posit both SCO and CO positions in the Church.

Jurisprudential Questions: Both the history of the just-war ethic and its application to the conditions of modern warfare illustrate the legitimacy of and the need for an SCO position. But the problems of traversing the ground from a desirable moral goal to an explicit legal position remain uncharted. There are both substantive and procedural issues involved: issues of determining the categories of SCO claims, and standards of fairness in determining the sincerity and rectitude of SCO positions taken by individuals.

Policy and Professional Questions: If SCO becomes an accepted option within the U.S. legal system, it will clearly have implications for policy and particularly for methods of procedure within the professional military. The policy consequences of legitimating an SCO option for citizens will involve a greater likelihood of a Vietnam-style debate about both ends and means of every conflict in which the government calls individuals to serve in the military. The nuclear debate—most of which takes place before any weapons are used—contains several possible SCO claims which individuals could make about specific targeting policies (counter-value) or weapons systems (a "first-strike" weapon) or strategic policies (launch-on-warning).

Within the military profession and the military bureaucracy specific attention would have to be paid to command questions in a world where SCO is an option for every member of the services.

Personal Questions: To invoke an SCO claim involves a more detailed and complex mode of reasoning than the conscientious objection position. Hence the bishops have on several occasions linked their teaching on war and on SCO with calls for moral education and conscience formation. The category of SCO will be unusable unless individuals have the requisite tools to argue issues of ends and means in warfare. To argue for SCO in the civil law is to call for a heightened capability for moral assessment in the body politic.

Both the bishops' position on SCO of the 1970s and their pastoral letter of 1983 are best seen as catalysts to further analysis, argument and advocacy on war and peace.

Notes

1. R.H. Bainton, *Christian Attitudes Toward War and Peace* (N.Y.: Abington Press, 1960).

2. L.B. Walters, *Five Classic Just-War Theories: A Study in the Thought of Thomas Aquinas, Vitoria, Suarez, Gentili and Grotius* (Unpublished Ph.D. Dissertation: Yale University, 1971), pp. 419–420.

3. In addition to Walters, cf: F.H. Russell, *The Just War in the Middle Ages* (London: Cambridge University Press, 1977); J. Johnson, *Ideology, Reason, and The Limitation of War: Religious and Secular Concepts, 1200–1740* (Princeton: Princeton University Press, 1975).

4. Russell (pp. 16–39) provides a synthetic statement of the theological and moral reasoning supporting Augustine's position.

5. Russell's argument is that Augustine provided theological grounding for Christian participation in war by "spiritualizing" the content of the Sermon on the Mount: it referred

to the inner disposition or intention of the Christian not principally to external actions, pp. 16–18.

6. Walters has taken the three criteria of Thomas and placed them within the larger framework of his ethical theory; none of the earlier commentators have provided such an extensive analysis of Aquinas' thought, pp. 69–199.

7. The treatment of self-defense by Thomas provided the first formulation of the rule of double-effect which then became a permanent feature of Catholic moral thought: *Summa Theologiae* II-II, q. 64; a. 7.

8. For the changing context in which Vitoria and Suarez wrote cf: J.T. Delos, "The Sociology of Modern War and The Theory of Just War," *Crosscurrents* (1958) 8: 248–65. For internal changes wrought in the ethical argument, cf: Walters, pp. 201–409 and Johnson, pp. 150–203.

9. For Grotius' contribution to just-war and international law cf: Walters; H. Lauterpacht, "The Grotian Tradition in International Law," *British Yearbook of International Law* 23 (1946).

10. J.C. Murray, "Remarks on the Moral Problem of War," *Theological Studies* (1959) 20: 40–61.

11. The theme of international order was a consistent dimension of Pius XII's teaching: cf: Christmas Address 1941, 1951, 1952, 1953 in V. Yzermans, ed., *Major Addresses of Pius XII*, vol. II (St. Paul: The North Central Publishing Co., 1961).

12. Murray, pp. 45–46; esp. fn. 12.

13. Murray makes the point that Pius XII was speaking to a particular situation, but the statement on conscientious objection seemed to have the force of a general principle for Pius XII; the text is the *Christmas Message* 1956; cited in Murray, p. 53.

14. The encyclicals of John XXIII, the conciliar text, and Pope Paul's Address to the United Nations are found in J. Gremillion, *The Gospel of Peace and Justice: Catholic Social Teaching Since John* (N.Y.: Orbis Books, 1976). Pope Paul also made a major statement each year on the occasion of The Day of Peace–an observance he initiated within the church.

15. This version is the way the text is translated in A. Flannery, *Vatican II: The Conciliar and Post-Conciliar Documents* (Collegeville: The Liturgical Press, 1975). Flannery is translating the *Pacem In Terris* paragraph as it is used in *Gaudium et Spes*, fn. to para. 80.

16. J. Douglass, *The Nonviolent Cross: A Theology of Revolution and Peace* (N.Y.: The Macmillan Co., 1966), p. 84.

17. P. Ramsey, *The Just War: Force and Political Responsibility* (N.Y.: Scribner's, 1968), p. 78.

18. *Gaudium et Spes*, para. 78; Gremillion, p. 315.

19. *Gaudium et Spes*, para. 79; Gremillion, p. 316.

20. Paul VI: *Message for Day of Peace* 1976.

21. Douglass asserts the nonviolent content of *Pacem In Terris* several times in his chapter "The Nonviolent Power of Pacem In Terris," p. 86; 94; 95.

22. J. Yoder, *Nevertheless: The Varieties of Religious Pacifism* (Scottsdale: Herald Press, 1971).

23. Pax Christi, *Some Moral Aspects of Disarmament*, Statement submitted to the Special Session of the U.N. on Disarmament; May-June 1978, p. 3.

24. *The Holy See and Disarmament* (Vatican City: Tipografia Poliglotta Vaticana, 1976).

25. *Gaudium et Spes*, para. 79; Gremillion, p. 316.

26. *Gaudium et Spes*, para. 81; Gremillion, p. 318.

27. *The Holy See and Disarmament*, p. 1, 2.

28. *Gaudium et Spes*, para. 82; Gremillion, p. 318.

29. *The Holy See and Disarmament*, p. 7; cf: *Pacem In Terris*, para. 112; Gremillion, p. 225.

30. The message of Paul VI to the U.N. Special Session on Disarmament exemplifies this balance; speaking of disarmament it said: "It seems to be a problem situated at the level of a prophetic vision, open to the hopes of the future. And yet one cannot really face this problem without remaining solidly based upon the hard and concrete reality of the present." (24 May 1978)

31. John Paul II, Address at Drogheda, Ireland, *Origins* (Oct. 11, 1979), p. 274.

32. John Paul II, *World Day of Peace Message* 1982, *Origins* (Jan. 7, 1982), p. 475.

33. Ibid. p. 478

34. Ibid.

35. *Gaudium et Spes*, para. 79; Gremillion, p. 315.

36. National Council of Catholic Bishops, "Human Life In Our Day," *Pastoral Letters of the United States Catholic Bishops* (Washington, D.C.: 1983), vol. III, p. 193 (cited hereafter as *Pastoral Letters*, with volume and page number).

37. United States Catholic Conference, "Declaration on Conscientious Objection and Selective Conscientious Objection," *Pastoral Letters*, vol. III, p. 285.

38. Ibid., p. 285.

39. Ibid., p. 286.

40. United States Catholic Conference, "Statement on Registration and Conscription for Military Service," *Pastoral Letters*, (Washington, D.C.: 1984), vol. IV, p. 361.

41. J.B. Hehir, "The Just-War Ethic and Catholic Theology," in T. Shannon, ed., *War or Peace? The Search for New Answers* (N.Y.: Orbis Books, 1980), pp. 15–39.

42. R.B. Potter, *The Moral Logic of War* (Philadelphia: United Presbyterian Church, n.d.); James Childress, "Just-War Theories," *Theological Studies*, (1978) 39: 427–45.

43. *The Challenge of Peace*, para. 121.

44. James Finn, "Pacifism and Just-War: Either or Neither," in P. Murnion, ed., *Catholics and Nuclear War* (N.Y.: Crossroads Publishers, 1983), pp. 142–43.

6

A Bishop Looks at Selective Conscientious Objection

Walter F. Sullivan

Other chapters have already reviewed the basic issues: The positive affirmation of selective conscientious objection by church officials is a morally acceptable position for the Christian and, for my purposes, the Roman Catholic. In my comments I want to develop some propositions which will, I hope, advance our dialogue.

The Catholic population as a whole has not accepted either universal or selective conscientious objection as part of Catholic teaching. U.S. Catholics are predominantly descendants of immigrants who came to this country in waves from 1850 to 1920. The newly arrived Catholics banded together for survival. They lived in the ghettos of larger cities. They experienced poverty, prejudice and oppression. They entered the work force at the lowest level. They found strength in numbers. As time passed, they began to make their presence felt educationally, politically and economically. They began to break down the barriers of discrimination. During this century's two world wars, Catholics proved that they were loyal Americans, patriotic to the core even though they belong to a world-wide church, headquartered in Rome. This upward mobility and progress toward social acceptance culminated in the election of a Catholic president in 1960.

For the American Catholic, patriotism was, and is, an important religious obligation. The Knights of Columbus established a 4th Degree which emphasized love of country. There are military high schools under Catholic auspices. Proportionally Catholics outnumber other religious groups in the military and in the service academies. For example, the 1986–87 student body of Virginia Military Institute (VMI) in Lexington, Virginia, is almost 50 percent Roman Catholic. I have known people to become indignant and enraged because a pastor, a young curate, a liturgy committee, or even a brash bishop removed the American flag from the church sanctuary.

Where do our Catholic people, on the whole, stand on the question of selective conscientious objection? We can learn something from the following personal experience, one which started me on my journey within the peace movement. I was ordained a bishop in December 1970. I soon discovered that bishops are called upon to share words of wisdom at all times and places. In the summer of 1971, at the height of the Vietnam War, I was invited to speak at an anniversary dinner of one of the diocese's most prestigious Knights of Columbus Councils. I chose as my topic, "Jesus, the Man of Peace." I spoke about the war and how people were becoming polarized. I even dared to point out that the church recognized conscientious objection as a choice an individual could conscientiously make. I found my audience getting restless. They went from indigestion to indignation. After the talk some of the Knights hurled epithets at me.

I was really shaken by the response. As I prepared to leave, a man with a distinctive crew cut came up and introduced himself as a Marine Sergeant. I said to myself, "nearer my God to thee." This unlikely ally in an audience of 400, though, said he wanted to thank me because tomorrow his son was leaving for Canada. He had been, he said, about to disown his son. He thanked me, because I had saved his son for him.

I share this story both because of its impact on me and because it made me realize how deep is the prejudice and even hate we bear toward anyone who seems disloyal to our country. The church indoctrinated us well with regard to the virtue of patriotism. We forget our roots as an oppressed, persecuted people and become intolerant of any of our sons who petition for conscientious objection status. I remember well the flak that was raised when, with our peace networks, I established draft counseling centers around the diocese and taught high school juniors and seniors about the formation of conscience. It seemed only right to bring this neglected teaching of our church into the religion classes of our schools and schools of religion. Many of our parents responded with their own very vocal display of conscientious objection. They charged me with indoctrinating our youth with liberal, pro-communist ideas.

I question whether the majority of our people even know the church's position on conscientious objection. I feel confident that, if they do, they do not agree or accept this teaching. Shortly after the bishops' pastoral letter on peace was released in 1983, our diocese surveyed its people on their attitudes toward peace. One survey item read: "Because of their faith Catholics should refuse to participate in waging a nuclear war." In 1983, 51.5 percent disagreed with that statement, while in 1986 47.6 percent disagreed. On both surveys only one-third of our people (33 percent) believed in selective conscientious objection to nuclear war. The people of the diocese have also become more pessimistic about the effects of nuclear war. In 1983 54 percent indicated that life would not be the same after nuclear war while in 1986, 62 percent held that view. As for agreeing with the bishops' position, 23 percent agreed with the U.S. bishops, 26 percent disagreed, and 45 percent had no opinion. The survey clearly shows that there is a real gap between the attitudes of Catholic people and the bishops' teaching. The hopeful sign, at least in Southern Virginia, is that a growing number of people are less sure of their opinions on questions of war and peace and have a growing concern over what a nuclear war would do to our world.

In summary, our Catholic people have made some progress since the days of the Vietnam War on issues such as conscientious objection, but we still have a monumental task before us in articulating our teaching and in gaining acceptance of that teaching by our Catholic people.

My second observation concerns the attitudes of those in charge of the Selective Service System. It is my conviction that they are fundamentally opposed to conscientious objection and especially to selective conscientious objection.

Federal law recognizes two types of conscientious objectors: persons who, by reason of deeply held moral, ethical or religious beliefs are conscientiously opposed to participating in war in any form; and persons holding the same beliefs who do not object to performing non-combatant duties (such as being a medic) in the armed forces. At the present time, federal law does not recognize selective conscientious objection despite the fact that the United States Catholic Conference made a strong endorsement of selective conscientious objection in 1971, when it urged "a modification of the Selective Service Act making it possible for selective conscientious objectors to refuse to serve in wars they consider unjust, without fear of imprisonment or loss of citizenship, provided they perform some other service to the human community." In the same statement, the USCC called for an end of peacetime conscription.

I have the privilege of serving on the board of NISBCO (the National Inter-religious Service Board for Conscientious Objectors) which is a coalition of 35 religious bodies formed to defend and to extend the rights of conscientious objectors. During the past several years NISBCO has had dialogue with the authorities of the Selective Service System. NISBCO has criticized the Selective Service System for not honoring or respecting the rights of conscientious objectors. The criticism cites, for example, the Selective Service System regulation which requires that draftees must apply for reclassification within ten days of the mailing of their draft notice. Furthermore, Selective Service at present does not supply information on the regulations to draftees who use their "hot line" to request it. Lists of people willing to advise registrants of the classification and induction process as well as the rights of draftees have been banned from Selective Service System area offices. Only a minuscule quantity of information booklets actually exist. Selective Service expects to reject two-thirds of conscientious objection claimants who make it through the existing process.

It is my conviction and that of NISBCO that a determined effort is being made to place roadblocks, contrary to the congressional intent to create an independent civilian agency, in the way of those seeking conscientious objection status. The

Selective Service System has shifted from civilian to military control under the Department of Defense. Selective Service has changed the long standing congressionally mandated arrangements for alternative service employers, thereby making it almost impossible for conscientious objectors to serve with traditional church sponsored employers. In November, 1981, I, along with Bishop Frank Murphy of Baltimore, Dr. Gordon Zahn of the Pax Christi Center on Conscience and War, and other concerned Catholics visited Major General Thomas K. Turnage, then Director of the Selective Service System. We were concerned because no Catholic dioceses or institutions were authorized to serve as alternative employers to conscientious objectors. Since then improvements have been made in the substance and tone of the Alternative Service proposals. At that same meeting, we also spoke about the need for a spirit of respect for the conscientious objector by local draft boards. During the Vietnam War I found that the members of draft boards, the people who have the initial say regarding conscientious objection status, were frequently hostile to those who for reasons of conscience refused to participate in war, especially in that particular war. I was told by some of these claimants that Catholics serving on local boards relied on the just war theory to prove that a Catholic could not in good conscience be opposed to all war.

NISBCO contributed substantially to the eventual rejection by the U.S. House of Representatives in 1986 of the regulations regarding conscientious objection set down by the Selective Service System. NISBCO vigorously objected to the "trick" questions to be asked of potential conscientious objectors in order to disqualify claimants. The questions in Form 22 made false distinctions between moral, ethical and religious claims. Each person would have had to pass a rigorous test in order to qualify for the exercise of the right to act in accord with conscience. My strongest objection to General Turnage in 1981 was the proposed use of religious "orthodoxy" or "devotional regularity" as a test of a registrant's sincerity in asserting his objection to war and military service. I believe that to raise a question relating to an individual's general religious views and behavior is a violation of the rights of the claimant and introduces matters which are outside the proper interest of Selective Service or of any draft board which may ultimately be put into operation. To question the "consistency" or "orthodoxy" of a registrant would open the doors for bias on the part of Catholic board members who are unfamiliar with the peace teachings and traditions of the Roman Catholic Church and who are likely to consider conscientious objection as less than fully orthodox.

Instead of revising the proposal, the Congress, by an overwhelming majority, rejected outright the suggested regulations for conscientious objection status. While the regulations may now be in limbo, the attitudes of those in charge of the program have not changed substantially. The Selective Service System has made a few concessions in the rules whereby conscientious objection claimants can postpone a military examination until after their hearing; local boards can review negative decisions on 4-F claims made by military examiners; and conscientious objection claimants have the right to a hearing if they miss the first scheduled hearing.

I am happy to report, however, a definite change in the attitude of Catholic chaplains who work with enlisted men whose conscience has crystallized since entering military service. I personally know of cases in the past where enlisted men have gone to three different chaplains who refused to counsel them. Now military commanders, rather than being vindictive, are open to those with post-induction claims for conscientious objection status because of sensitive assignments and security risks. Our diocese presently has a seminarian who realized only after volunteering for the military that he could not in conscience participate or cooperate in a nuclear exchange. Thanks to the head chaplain the young man could leave the military in dignity rather than in disgrace. The military has now officially recognized that it is to its advantage to dismiss conscientious objectors and to term the process "conscience crystallization."

So far I have attempted to show that our Catholic people on the whole do not agree with church teaching on conscientious objection and selective conscientious objection and that frequently those associated with the Selective Service System do whatever they can to prevent a registrant from obtaining conscientious objection status. Must we not conclude that we have much to do if the rights of conscience are to be recognized and respected? In view of the attitudes of our own Catholic people, of society at large, and of the authorities of the Selective Service System toward conscientious objectors (whom we label "draft dodgers") I would like to propose some pastoral responses.

1. We must step up our educational efforts among our people and, especially, among the young of draft age regarding the primacy of conscience and on the obligation of conscience either to join the armed forces or to seek conscientious objection status.

2. We should oppose a peace-time draft. I mention this because one hears the claim that the U.S. needs to reinstate the draft so we can increase our military presence in Europe in the event that medium range missiles are removed by both sides, leaving Russia with a vast superiority in conventional forces.

3. Dioceses should have standby plans for draft counseling centers with training personnel in preparation for a possible re-establishment of the draft. The Pax Christi Center on Conscience and War could serve as an excellent resource for the development of centers and for the training of counselors. Dioceses should also monitor the selection of persons to serve on local draft boards and inform board members of present-day Catholic teaching on issues of war and peace.

4. Religious groups and concerned citizens should continue to scrutinize the regulations set down by the Selective Service System. I certainly favor civilian control of Selective Service and the elimination of bias against conscientious objectors and those who work in their behalf. Selective Service System representatives have refused to meet with NISBCO and in fact describe the leader of

NISBCO, William Yolton, as "mean spirited." I also favor a much broader interpretation of alternative service to include institutions and programs under religious auspices.

5. It is particularly important to continue efforts to obtain legal recognition for selective conscientious objection. From its support for traditional just war teaching, some conclude that the Church does not rule out all wars as immoral. As a result, a Catholic young person who accepts Catholic teaching but who conscientiously rejects a particular war as immoral now has to choose between going to prison or violating conscience. Pope John Paul II at Coventry, England declared that "the scale and horror of modern war—whether nuclear or not—makes it totally unacceptable as a means of settling differences between and among nations." On several occasions since 1976 the U.S. Catholic Bishops have called for changes in the present law in order to recognize conscience—opposition to participation in or training for, any war, that in the individual's moral judgment, does not meet the conditions of the "just war." The official refusal by Selective Service System to permit conscientious objection to a particular war is, in my opinion, a denial of freedom of religion.

Since the Catholic Church distinguishes between "just" and "unjust" wars, members of that church should not be penalized or treated differently from members of the traditional "peace churches" which reject all wars. While the U.S. Catholic bishops have spoken in favor of the inviolability of conscience and of the right of conscientious objection and selective conscientious objection, Catholic teaching on peace, non-violence and conscientious objection still remains the best kept secret in the Catholic Church.

6. Bishops should dialogue with representatives of the Military Archdiocese and, on the local level, with the Catholic chaplains located in their dioceses. I have found a growing spirit of cooperation among chaplains and local clergy and parish staffs. The time is ripe to encourage dialogue on issues of conscience. I am certain that chaplains are encountering a growing number of enlisted men whose idealism or adventurism is shaken and challenged by the reality of modern warfare. At a time of questioning, hopefully a service man or woman will be able to turn to a priest, military or civilian, and receive a sympathetic hearing rather than rejection as "unpatriotic" or as a "peacenik."

We must help young people make mature and moral choices among the options open to them with respect to military service. Our task is not to persuade anyone to serve or not to serve. We must, though, remind young people that whatever course they decide to follow, their decision must be a moral choice, the product of mature deliberation and subject always to the primacy of conscience. As we prepare young people in conscientious moral decision making, we must at the same time provide the legal avenues whereby those decisions will be treated with dignity, without threat of loss of face or job opportunities or, worse still, the prospect of imprisonment.

As Thomas Merton reminded us:

Speaking in the name of Christ and of the Church to all of humankind, Pope John (in *Pacem in Terris*) was not issuing a pacifist document in this sense. He was not simply saying that if a few cranks did not like the bomb they were free to entertain their opinion. He was saying, on the contrary, that we had reached a point in history where it was clearly no longer reasonable to make use of war in the settlement of disputes, and that the important thing was not merely protest against the latest war technology, but the construction of permanent world peace on a basis of truth, justice, love and liberty. This is not an individual refinement of spirituality, a luxury of the soul, but a collective obligation of the highest urgency, a universal and immediate need which can no longer be ignored.

7

The Good of Selective
Conscientious Objection

John P. Langan

What is the good of selective conscientious objection? Why is it a good? And for whom is it a good? These questions may seem to be a strange way to open a chapter reflecting on the morality of selective conscientious objection for at least two reasons. In the first place, we think of conscientious objection as a negative way of responding to evils rather than as a good to be attained or striven for. The context for principles and decisions in this matter is violent and coercive. That which is to be decided is participation or nonparticipation in war, the most sanguinary and destructive of human activity. That which impels to decision is the legal demand, backed by the coercive power of the state, that all those judged to be qualified by the state must, if called, participate in this activity which requires the doing and suffering, the awaiting and the threatening of great evils. Note here that I am speaking of evils in a pre-moral sense which does not imply that a negative answer has already been given to the question of whether war in general or any given war is morally justifiable but which does bring with it a strong need for moral justification.

In the absence of such justification, however, the case for the moral condemnation of war is short and compelling. The decision to participate in this questionable activity is itself what William James spoke of as a "genuine option," one that is "living, forced, and momentous."[1] At least, this is the case for those who are in the class of persons being drafted for military service. The connection between being drafted and being required to participate in war or in combat activities is close but not invariable. A person may be drafted with a view to serving in a particular war which is going on or which is imminent. But the likelihood of actually serving in combat varies, depending on a number of factors: the person's physical and mental condition, the fit or lack of it between the person's skills and the needs of the military services, and command decisions about the deployment of forces and of

89

individual personnel. However, the majority of persons in the armed services have
to reckon with the possibility of serving in combat. Even if they do not do so, they
have to consider the likelihood that they will be assisting those who do. It is both
unrealistic and irresponsible for those called to serve in the military to ignore these
possibilities or to fail to scrutinize their moral aspects, precisely because the
activity of carrying on war is both morally questionable and personally troubling.

The object of decision, when one deals with conscientious objection either in a
selective or comprehensive form, is a social activity with major negative aspects;
and this should never be forgotten. At the same time the context for the decision is
itself coercive. It is not like the making of consumer decisions about one's
disposable income. The decision comes with an externally imposed timetable and
with threats of punishment for noncompliance or noncooperation, in the case of
those being drafted. The context is also coercive, though in different ways when a
person already in the armed services makes the decision. To enter into the process
of deliberation itself about the decision exposes a person to social pressures and to
the prospect of sanctions, both formal and informal, and to potentially severe
internal conflicts. I stress the negative aspects of the context of the decision, not as
part of a plea for change but as a recognition of what I take to be inherent features
of the situation, even though all of them do not have the character of logical
necessity. Even if we discover selective conscientious objection to be a good, it
will be somewhat like a wildflower springing up in an Alpine environment, and we
may be tempted to ask Moliere's question of Scapin, "What were you doing in that
gallery?"[2]

The second reason for not thinking of selective conscientious objection as a
good is that we may be inclined to think of it more as a right, a claim not to be
interfered with in making a decision of a certain kind. The connections between
rights and goods form a complex topic which different philosophical and theological traditions have handled in different ways. But very often in those legal and
philosophical traditions which have been dominant in the United States, the notion
of right has been understood as a liberty which may be used well or ill and which
is not necessarily tied to a good. The stress is on freedom from interference or
coercion or mistreatment.[3] Thus, people will speak of the right to smoke, the right
to an abortion, the right to maintain false beliefs, the right to engage in homosexual
activity, and so on. Rights or liberties are to be restricted or denied only when the
exercise of them produces harm to other persons, as in the case of shouting "Fire!"
in a crowded theater.[4] The affirmation of rights in this sense does not imply moral
endorsement of the actions of persons who exercise their rights; and it does not
mandate the active cooperation of other persons in assisting those who exercise
their rights to achieve the goals or the goods that they seek. The affirmation of
rights understood in this predominantly negative way,[5] is nicely captured in
Voltaire's dictum that "I disagree with what you say, but I will defend to the death
your right to say it."[6] This way of understanding rights usually goes with a concern

for restricting the powers of the state, which is normally the single most powerful source of interference with the exercise of rights; and it is often accompanied by a high level of agnosticism about goods, especially goods that are regarded as obligatory or as worthy of being pursued by public policy or collective action.[7] This view of rights has been prevalent in liberal political philosophy and has been widely attractive in a pluralistic and pragmatic society of the sort that we have in the United States. But it is worth observing that other philosophical traditions, notably utilitarianism and Aristotelian realism, have begun with a stress on the goods to be pursued by human action and have accorded only a secondary place, if that, to rights in their development of moral theory and in their understanding of a good society.

Conscientious objection in general and selective conscientious objection in particular seem to be inherently contentious matters on which we cannot reasonably expect that all men and women of good will or all those who approach the question from the moral point of view are likely to agree. The issue of conscientious objection brings to the front of our attention certain tensions between traditional values and current experience, between public policy and personal aspiration, between secular and religious conceptions of community which we do not have a standard procedure for resolving. It is also an issue on which society and participants in the debate are likely to alternate between urgent concern when the bullets are flying and negligent apathy when there is no proximate prospect of hostilities. So we may well be inclined to think that the most we can do in this area is to see our task as setting the limits of a right which will enable us to act according to our personal judgment without consensus on the major values or goods which are present in the debate. I believe that we can and should do more than that.

As basic reference points for an examination of this problem I will take two documents, the pastoral constitution of the Second Vatican Council on the Church and the Modern World, *Gaudium et Spes* (1965) and the 1967 report of the U.S. National Advisory Commission on Selective Service, commonly referred to by the name of its chairman as *The Marshall Report*.[8] These offer reference points for a debate that raises universal issues of principle but that is specifically American and religious in its focus and its characteristic range of considerations and solutions.

The general stance taken by the Vatican on questions of war and peace is especially important because it provides the authoritative intellectual basis for many of the subsequent papal and episcopal pronouncements in this area, notably the 1983 pastoral letter of the U.S. Catholic bishops, *The Challenge of Peace*. The crucial points that are relevant to selective conscientious objection are:

1. the right of governments to legitimate defense, given the present structure of the international order;[9]

2. the insistence that not every political or military use of force is "lawful" or morally justified;

3. the affirmation that those in military service are to "regard themselves as agents of security and freedom;"

4. the condemnation of actions and orders that violate the principles of "universal natural law;"

5. praise for courageous resistance to orders violating these principles;

6. the binding force of international agreements "aimed at making military activity and its consequences less inhuman;"

7. endorsement of laws that "make humane provisions for the case of those who for reasons of conscience refuse to bear arms, provided however, that they accept some other form of service to the human community;"

8. praise for those "who renounce the use of violence in the vindication of their rights and who report to methods of defense which are otherwise available to weaker parties, provided that this can be done without injury to the rights and duties of others or of the community itself."[10]

These points are embedded within a generally negative attitude to war and to the new and frightful forms of violence which have developed in the recent past. They provide a normative direction which recognizes the present division of political and military power among a plurality of distinct political communities, some of which can pose a threat to the security and freedom of others, but which at the same time maintains an aspiration for a new form of international order in which an effective authority would reconcile conflicts without violence and would direct all peoples to the realization of the international common good. The elimination and outlawing of war, though clearly an urgently desirable goal, is not the immediate task. Rather, at the present time there is a moral obligation to put aside "enmities and hatred" and to reach "honest agreements" about world peace and disarmament.[11] The teaching of the Vatican Council focuses primarily on the social and political context for the use of violence, rather than on the decisions of individuals that are the normal staple of traditional casuistry. The innovative aspect of the Council's teaching consists mainly in its concern for the transformation of this context, a transformation which is an inherently political task but which is undertaken in response to moral concerns. The Council does not reject traditional approaches to the moral assessment of war, but it is mainly interested in calling Christians and persons of good will to deal with new problems. It holds that in this area, as in so many other areas of theology and ethics, merely repeating old answers to old questions, even while these answers are correct, is insufficient to shape a full Christian response to the needs of the modern world.

The teaching of Vatican II is not without what some would regard as utopian aspirations; but at the same time it does not discard the continuing place of just-war theory in the formation of moral judgment about contemporary problems of violence and war. Just-war theory, when it is treated as a source of guidance for the formation of judgments of conscience in concrete situations, is best seen as a kind of red-flashing traffic light. It calls not merely for caution but for a reflective stop before proceeding. The theory is itself not a simple listing of precepts, prohibitions, and permissions such that one can look at the normative statement and at the proposed action and then draw a moral conclusion about what is or is not to be done. Rather, it calls for acts of judgment about the situation seen as a complex whole.

The theory has a kind of "yes-but" structure to it which makes its application to particular cases complex and indeterminate. Thus, it says in effect:

- Yes, peace is to be preferred, but war may be justified under certain circumstances.

- Yes, war is justifiable, but only if certain restrictions are observed.

- Yes, war is justified by certain values, but these values are not to be identified with the winning of the war or with prevailing over the enemy.

- Yes, commands of military superiors are to be obeyed, but not if they exceed certain moral limits.

- Yes, the enemy may rightly be killed, but only under certain circumstances and with a certain attitude or frame of mind.

- Yes, violence is a legitimate instrument for attaining some supremely important political ends, but it is never a neutral or indifferent instrument.

Because of this structure, just-war theory is not to be identified with either pacifism or militarism. It yields only a conditioned approval for acts of violence. The conclusions reached in applying just-war theory to particular situations do not normally have the definiteness that can be found in pacifist or statist arguments that proceed from such premises as the moral wrongness of taking life or using violence or the moral obligation of obeying the orders of established authority. The application of such standard criteria of just-war theory as proportionality, comparative justice, resort to force only as a last resort, reasonable prospect of success, clearly involves complex judgments for which precise criteria cannot be given.

This indeterminacy is applying the norms of just-war theory is not, of course, the whole story. Some norms, as for instance the prohibition of killing non-combatants, or the principle of discrimination, clearly rule out such actions as the My Lai massacre or the bombing of Dresden. But even when we are dealing with a straight-forward prohibition, and where it is clear that civilians have been killed, there are likely to be significant gray areas which are relevant for our moral evaluation and response. For instance, there can be questions about whether the civilian deaths were intended or not, whether they were inflicted as part of a necessary military mission, whether they occurred as an isolated incident or as part of a systemic breakdown of standards or as the expression of a deliberate policy. It may seem that I am overdoing matters by all this talk of complexity and indeterminacy. Surely, some wars have been fought, and some deeds have been performed in the course of various wars that have been so evil, so lacking in plausible and honest moral justification that one should have no hesitation in condemning them. I do not disagree with this claim, nor do I wish to encourage people to take refuge in insoluble complexity in order to evade the necessity for decision. Rather, what one needs to take with equal seriousness is the fact that large numbers of men and women of good will, of sound character and serious judgment, read situations of armed conflict in different ways and draw different moral conclusions.

I am, also engaging in the philosopher's analytic task of uncovering the structure of common sense judgments. Our ability to "smell a rat" usually does not depend on our consciously deploying an elaborate theoretical apparatus. But when we try to explain why we smell a rat or to organize our judgments about the various rats we have smelled, then the task does become complex. "Intuition" in some broad sense is indeed an important guide for people in their conduct of the business of life. At the same time, as rational beings sharing in the rational institution of morality and engaging in the continuing civil conversation, we are impelled to give reasons for the moral judgments we make and the decisions we take. The challenges of explaining why we differ in our judgments from other persons in positions of authority or with greater experience, and of accounting for how we decide some cases one way and others another push us in the direction of building a rationale or a theory. This theory may be more or less articulate or adequate. But the pressure to move to more fine-grained rationales and criteria is inherent whenever we are dealing with a general class of actions which contains some members that seem clearly wrong, others that seem clearly right, and still others about which we are uncertain. The complexity and indeterminacy of just-war theory is just what we should expect when we systematize our judgments about an aspect of our common life that has been historically significant and controversial and that continues to be morally perplexing and troubling.

But what is the bearing of all this complexity and indeterminacy on the problem of selective conscientious objection? There are three points of contrast and potential difficulty. In the first place, just-war theory (and the just-war tradition) which encompasses many revisions and developments of just-war norms and their basic rationales, is the construction of generations of lawyers, philosophers, theologians and reflective warriors. The decisions taken by would-be selective conscientious objectors are taken by young men who have not reached full maturity of character and judgment and who are, in many cases, not particularly well educated or well informed.

Second, just-war theory deals with public considerations. They are not observable in the way that positivists and empiricists would like; but they are, with the exception of the requirement of right intention, not much concerned with the mysteries and yearnings of the human heart. The application of just-war norms does not presuppose, for the making of the argument, the possession of exceptional virtue or imagination or sensitivity in the persons who are reflecting on the problem. Just-war theory does not provide a test or a criterion for the motives of those who rely on it for guidance; nor can it resolve the often painful doubts about his own motives that are likely to trouble a conscientious objector except by pointing him toward the public considerations of justice such as proportionality, or the treatment of combatants and non-combatants. This does not mean that the application of just-war theory to particular situations may not be corrupted by base or cowardly motives or by prejudices that can involve both intellectual blindness and moral fault. Nor does it mean that carrying out decisions arrived at after deliberation using just-war norms does not require courage, commitment, and moral character. Just-war theory because of its public and rational character, is quite limited in meeting many of the personal needs and dilemmas that are felt by the young men who are drawn to consider the possibility of conscientious objection. I suggest that the actual outcome of applying just-war theory to a particular military situation will depend on just how this application is set within the context of a counseling or advocacy situation, and more particularly on how the "burden of proof" is defined and assigned. The evaluation of the use of force in terms of just-war theory involves a mode of moral reasoning and assessment which is quite different from privatized and highly personalized conceptions of conscience in which a "still, small voice" delivers absolute judgments for which no reason can be assigned.

The third point of contrast to be kept in mind is that between the range of disciplined judgments about the use of force which just-war theory enables us to make and the points of decision that confront those who must determine whether or not they are to be selective conscientious objectors to a particular war. I said "points of decision," in the plural because the basic pattern of moral assessment, deliberation, and decision in these matters seems to be the same whether the question arises prior to a person's being summoned for military service or for registration or whether it arises during the course of military service, although the specific pressures and uncertainties that may influence a person's decision and the experiences and particular considerations which a person draws on in his deliberations may alter in many ways. But it seems that in all cases the bottom-line answer is: yes or no to active participation in a particular war or use of military force. The no and the yes can be based on considerations specific to the war or on more general considerations. This bottom-line answer is either-or, though the forms of participation may vary and ways may be sought to evade or to soften the harshness of this disjunction. But the application of just-war theory offers a wider range of moral judgments than this, and the precise bearing of these judgments on the decision to participate or not is less than fully clear.

As an example of what I have in mind, I pose a problem which arises from the division of just-war theory into two distinct segments, one of which (the *jus ad bellum*) is concerned with answering the question of whether it is justifiable for a state to take up arms against an adversary while the second (the *jus in bello*) is concerned with maintaining respect for the norms of justice in the course of hostilities. Suppose then a case in which a person believes that his country meets the tests of the *jus ad bellum* (competent authority, just cause, right intention, last resort, comparative justice, reasonable prospect of success, and proportionality), but he also believes that in its conduct of hostilities it is seriously violating the norms of the *jus in bello* (proportionality and discrimination). He is then confronted with a dilemma—is it right for him to give up the just cause, the justice of the end aimed at in the conduct of the war because of the injustice of the means? The range of this dilemma can be restricted somewhat by observing that a soldier or officer should not participate directly in morally wrong activity, such as the unwarranted killing of civilians. If the avoidance of this kind of evil were the only value at stake, then no dilemma would arise; and the right course of action would clearly be to avoid participation in the war. On the other hand, if the justice of the cause were the only value at stake, then also no dilemma would arise; and participation would be right and mandatory. More specifically, consider the case of a person who believes that it is obligatory to resist the monstrous evils of the Nazi regime and to do what he can to rescue the victims of such a tyrannical regime. The only effective way to do this is to join in the war effort. On the other hand, the war effort itself is corrupted by indiscriminate bombing attacks on civilian population centers. The theorist can rest content with the observation that the war is just in its origins and unjust in its actual conduct. The advocate or critic can urge that the policy of indiscriminate bombing be changed so that the conduct of the war may be made just. But the serving solider, the enlistee or draftee is confronted with an either-or decision once the issue is posed in these terms.

One classical way of resolving this problem goes back to Aquinas's concise maxim: "bonum ex integra causa, malum ex quocumque defectu." The meaning of this maxim is simply that an action is good when all its essential elements are good or acceptable, when it is in this sense integral or complete, and that it is bad whenever any aspect of it is defective or bad. In contemporary philosophical terminology, this point can be made by stating that the various conditions for the rightness of an action (as laid down, for instance, in the norms of just-war theory) are individually necessary and jointly sufficient. In some ways, this seems to be a counsel of perfection for actions. It is certainly true that any defect or negative aspect of an action is reason for not performing the action. But it clearly seems to be the case that many of the actions that we perform have negative aspects and that we still perform them because we believe that they are right or justifiable. This holds true for the characteristic uses of force in military combat to destroy the military assets of the adversary. So it seems that principle should not be taken in a perfectionist sense. If it is not taken in a perfectionist sense, which would rule out any actions with negative consequences, then by itself it does not rule out the possibility of participating in a larger action or series of actions which has negative and questionable aspects. Traditional moral theology, when it considered the determinants of the goodness of an action (the object, the end, and the circumstances) treated the end in a way which made it agent-relative so that it did not determine the morality of a class of actions performable by many different agents. It focused rather on the object which was the formal principle of action, specifying what kind of thing was being done, and which was for certain types of actions held to vitiate them so radically that the actions were never justifiable. But this view was not adopted with regard to such centrally important actions as the taking of human life or the deception of adversaries. If the object is not condemned as wrong in all possible situations, then it seems that the circumstances of the actions must be examined, and some sort of comparative assessment of positive and negative circumstances needs to be undertaken. Among these circumstances the consequences of the action are of central, though not unique, importance. Once again, we are left with indeterminacy in the application of just-war norms.

The special form of this indeterminacy can be briefly stated: at what point does evil in the conduct of a war require that a person not participate in a war? This indeterminacy does not leave a person free to participate directly in actions that are clearly seen to be morally wrong or that are violations of the laws of war. But it arises with regard to participation in a war that is taken to be substantially just but that is partially corrupted by morally wrong actions. The soldier's or draftee's decision to serve is fundamentally a decision to serve in the armed forces at a given time and more specifically to take part in the waging of a particular war or use of force at that time. That is too broad a decision in its scope to be fully determined by negative or positive judgments about the morality of particular acts of war. The fundamental reason for this sort of indeterminacy is that war is not a simple action but is a complex series of actions.

There are two principal ways of resolving this indeterminacy. The first involves a judgment that the wrong or negative actions involved in the carrying out of the war are simply too numerous to be outweighed by the justice of the cause and by the judgment that the conditions of the *jus ad bellum* have been met. Such a judgment might reasonably be made about an extended conventional war in Europe against Soviet forces in which disproportionate numbers of civilian casualties would result. Appealing to the norm of proportionality in such a case would, however, replace one form of indeterminacy by another. Reasons can be given for such a judgment, and it is not purely arbitrary; but it is not something we can reasonably expect all people of good will to agree on, even if they accept just-war norms as the criteria of judgment. The second way of resolving the indeterminacy is to conclude that the wrong or negative actions are so intimately connected with the attainment of the objectives of the war or with the general direction of the war that the war either cannot be prosecuted in a just manner or that it will not in fact be so prosecuted. The wrong actions are judged to be not simply aberrations, e.g., an isolated massacre of civilians or a bombing raid on a civilian target, actions which are to be condemned in themselves but which do not vitiate the entire war effort. Rather, the judgment is that the wrong actions are somehow essential to the war effort and that therefore the war will not be waged in a just manner. If, for instance, a government assumes that the only way to bring a guerrilla war to a successful conclusion is to depopulate entire areas of the country and judges that it cannot afford to make provision for the safeguarding of civilian lives in the area in question. A judgment that a just cause cannot be defended by just means or even that it is not being defended by just means has a tragic character to it and is not to be lightly made. But in a sinful world in which right and might are not nicely aligned with each other such judgments will have to be made from time to time. We need only look at the situation of Poland over the last fifty years for some idea of what such judgments might mean. The possibility of tensions and conflicts between the worth of the ends and the moral rightness or wrongness of the means is built into the structure of just-war theory and cannot in principle be eliminated.

In what has proceeded, I have been particularly concerned with the difficulties and indeterminacies which arise within any serious effort to apply just-war norms to contemporary conflicts, since this is the normative framework for Catholic thinking on this problem and since it is the expectation both of the Church's authoritative teachers and of many of its members that these norms should be used in the assessment of military policy and action. Catholics along with non-Catholics, do not regard appeal to these norms as an effort to impose a set of sectarian constraints on the actions of other free citizens but as the expression of human rationality when confronted with the responsibility of making conscientious decisions about the use of force and so as norms which should be seen as binding for all. The possibility of selective conscientious objection is built into the structure of just-war theory at least in the sense that it always contains the possibility of judging that a particular war is not morally justifiable because it fails to meet one or more of the norms laid down in the theory and that therefore an individual applying the theory will judge that it is not morally right for him or her to participate in the war, at least as a combatant. It is therefore possible to interpret the denial of legal recognition to selective conscientious objectors as an objection to reliance on the norms of just-war theory in general or to their use by individuals, especially those who are liable to military service.

Here it is appropriate to turn to our other reference point for our reflections on this topic, namely, *The Marshall Report* of 1967, which recommended against according legal status to selective conscientious objectors. The National Advisory Commission on Selective Service was divided on the matter, with the majority taking the view that "conscientious objection must be based on opposition to war in all forms."[12] The majority of the Commission rejected a minority proposal that would have allowed selective conscientious objectors to be excused from combatant service but would have required them to "serve in a non-combatant military capacity, under conditions of hardship and even of hazard, and perhaps for a longer period (for example, three years)."[13] Five reasons—which turn out to be six—are offered for rejecting the minority proposal.

First, the majority argued that it is "one thing to deal in law with a person who believes he is responding to a moral imperative outside of himself when he opposes all killing" and "another to accord a special status to a person who believes there is a moral imperative which tells him he can kill under some circumstances and not kill under others."[14] On one level, this is trivially true. It is also true that, as Thomas Aquinas points out, it is not appropriate for all evil acts to be forbidden by law or for all good acts to be required by law. There are very good reasons for keeping distinction between law and morality, even though these two central institutions of our social life overlap in their contents and in many of the values they inculcate. But, in dealing with issues of military service and conscientious objection, we are not dealing with an area of private activity which can be argued to be beyond the appropriate range of governmental activity or with an area of intimate personal relations in which legal coercion is an unwarranted intrusion. Rather, we are dealing with a problem one of whose constituent elements is a demand by government itself on the citizen. It may still be true that the "one thing" may be more easily and more clearly resolved by administrative or judicial action than the other. The difficulties of implementing a procedure for resolving in a fair and honest manner the problems created by recognition of selective conscientious objection may be great. They may even be so great that they prevent us from acknowledging in law distinctions which many from the Protestant, Catholic, and Jewish traditions would recognize as holding in morality. But this is a case that needs to be made in much more detail and that needs to be evaluated carefully by experts and assessed by the public and its representatives. It is also true that just-war theory contains large elements of indeterminacy which make its application to particular cases much less straightforward than the application of a single negative norm which is accorded overriding importance. This undoubtedly complicates the legal task of designing a general procedure and of assessing individual decisions; but it does not present insuperable difficulties.

The Commission then went on to offer a further consideration against the minority, observing that "the question of 'classical Christian doctrine' on the subject of just and unjust-wars is one which would be interpreted in different ways by different Christian denominations and therefore not a matter upon which the Commission could pass judgment."[15] This is undoubtedly correct, but it has little relevance to the issue at hand. It would, of course, be a great mistake to base legal recognition of selective conscientious objection on a claim that an interpretation of just-war theory which includes this feature is a correct theological development of Christian tradition or is an adequate expression of the moral demands of Christian faith. Such a basis for law would involve a violation of the separation of church and state on two counts, since it would involve a governmental body in passing on matters in theological dispute and since it would offer a religious rationale for governmental action, a rationale which would be inappropriate to the secular purposes of government and offensive to those from other religious traditions or with other theological perspectives. But the point at issue is the fact that many Christians and some others would form their consciences along lines suggested by some form of the just-war tradition, or at least that they should do so if they are faithful to the teaching of their religious communities. The point is for the government to show respect for the conscience and for the religious freedom of these persons, not for it to pronounce on disputed theological questions.

The majority of the Commission offered as its second reason that "so-called selective pacifism is essentially a political question of support or non-support of a war and cannot be judged in terms of special moral imperatives." They went on to observe that "political opposition to a particular war should be expressed through recognized democratic processes and should claim no special right of exemption from democratic decisions."[16] This last observation is not without merit. But it comes close to giving the game away; for it makes it plain that the operative paradigm for the Commission's understanding of moral judgment is of the general pattern: X is a wrong or forbidden type of action under all circumstances and is not to be done. The underlying conception of morality is of a system of exceptionless deontological norms. Now such a conception has had a certain hold over large parts of our popular culture; but it would be easy to show that it coexists with a much more pragmatic openness to exceptions and that it is rejected by large numbers of philosophical and theological moralists coming from diverse intellectual and religious traditions. It is this underlying conception of morality with its paradigm of moral judgment that makes it possible for the Commission to dismiss judgments involving the application of just-war norms as political rather than moral.

It is true that there is a certain overlap between political judgments and moral judgments arrived at from the standpoint of just-war theory. Just war considerations such as the legitimacy of authority, the proportionality of means to ends, and the likelihood of success should all show up in intelligent political assessments of the use of force and the application of just-war norms is more complex and indeterminate than the simple invocation of an absolute or exceptionless norm. But this complexity should be seen as part of an adequate moral assessment of the complexity of political-military affairs. Whether one thinks of just-war theory in terms of its historic role in the expression of Christian moral teaching about warfare or in terms of such contemporary notions as the moral point of view, the just-war theory must be seen as a system for making moral judgments—judgments which remain moral even when they take account of political considerations precisely because they allow for judgments which may not be in accordance with the political interests of individuals or of particular states. It is mistaken for the Commission to dismiss the application of just-war theory as political. It is also mistaken to contrast universal conscientious objection and selective conscientious objection as moral and political, as the Commission implicitly does, and then to treat the latter, but not the former, as involving a "special right of exemption from democratic decisions." Rather, the failure to recognize selective conscientious objection means that unequal and unfair treatment is given to those who form their consciences about military matters along the lines of absolutist pacifism and along the lines proposed by just-war theory. The law exempts one group from the burdens imposed by democratic decisions and not the other. This is unfair and unjust and threatens the religious liberty of those who would form their consciences according to the norms of just-war theory.

The third reason which the Commission offers for rejecting the minority view is that legal recognition of selective conscientious objection would "open the doors to a general theory of selective disobedience to law, which could quickly tear down the fabric of government."[17] This is a view which partly reflects the anxiety produced by the practice of civil disobedience within the civil rights movement and the emergence of various forms of revolutionary and radical protest in the late 1960s. It is also a form of "slippery slope" argument, which relies on a mixture of normative considerations and empirical claims about social psychology. "Slippery slope" arguments cannot be dismissed out of hand since they can point to important costs and dangers of changing social policy. But, precisely because of their predictive element, they have to be recognized as less than conclusive. More specifically, this particular "slippery slope" argument misses the point. Permitting selective conscientious objection would reduce the number of cases of civil obedience, whereas refusal to recognize selective conscientious objection will increase the numbers of those who believe that they must disobey the law in order to obey their consciences or the will of God. Selective conscientious objection can be seen as a response in accordance with the law, though it is not in accordance with the policy of the state. But in our kind of polity the law is not simply to be equated with the policy of the state.

The Commission attempted to bolster this line of argument with the claim that "the distinction is dim between a person conscientiously opposed to participation in a particular war and one conscientiously opposed to payment of a particular tax." In response to this, one can observe that while the line between war and the authorized use of force by the state may not always be easy to draw, as, for instance, in the "police action" in Korea in the early 1950s, or in the later intervention in Grenada, there seems to be little difficulty in distinguishing the use of force against external adversaries from other activities of the government. It is so precisely because of our general ability to make this distinction and our recognition of the special moral gravity of requiring other people to actively engage in processes that will kill other people. It is true that moral objections could also be raised against a wide range of government activities and that many of these objections could be motivated by selfish and self-protective desires to avoid one's due share of the burdens, sacrifices, and risks which are imposed by our life together as citizens. For these reasons conscientious objection, whether in a universal or selective form, is not extended to all those things that individuals coming from diverse backgrounds and traditions might find morally troubling (for instance, the Amish objection to being photographed). Care is taken to determine whether the objector's motives are conscientious or interested. It is significant that the fact that a refusal to serve in combat is probably in a person's interest narrowly conceived is not allowed to determine our judgment of his motivation but does prompt us to raise the question and to scrutinize answers carefully. Concern over the socially destructive effects of unrestrained selfishness was prominent in the thought of our Founding Fathers and is one of the commonest themes in our public discourse. There is a public interest in putting the objector's motivation under scrutiny.

At the same time, our public philosophy does not impose on us the acceptance of some form of psychological egoism but allows for a wider range of motives, among which are religious and moral considerations. There is also a public interest in showing respect for freedom of conscience, especially on matters of fundamental importance, an interest which is connected with our character as a pluralistic, free, and stable society. As a society we take a double stance on conflicts between the democratic state and the conscientious individual. We restrict the power of the state and uphold a theory of limited government; at the same time, we require that the decisions of the government be obeyed when they are within the range of matters it is competent to settle. The provision of national defense and the conduct of war is clearly one of these matters. For the government to honor the conscientious objections of some citizens in this area is in accordance with the fundamental value of respect for freedom for belief and conscience. But it is right for this exception to be limited to the particularly grave and troubling matter of participation in combat.

This brings us close to the fourth of the Commission's reasons for opposing selective conscientious objection, namely, its inability "to see the morality of a proposition which would permit the selective pacifist to avoid combat service by performing noncombatant service in support of a war which he had theoretically concluded to be unjust."[18] In one sense, this is clearly right. If the war is unjust, participation in it is wrong whether one serves as a combatant or a noncombatant. But this argument overlooks two key points. In this hypothetical situation of a putatively unjust-war, there is also an assumption that the government along with significant numbers of the citizens have judged the war to be just. While there are conscientious objectors, there are also conscientious participants. There is a point which conscientious objectors themselves should be brought to recognize and to affirm. Some moral critics of government policy and military action have been too easily content with characterizations of those who disagree with them as conformists or militarists or persons devoid of moral sensitivity and concern. Law and public policy should be framed so as to recognize this diversity of judgments and to affirm the legitimate and necessary power of government over the citizens in conducting the national defense. In a situation where a responsible government recognizes selective conscientious objection but imposes a requirement of noncombatant service in the military or some other form of national service, it does not concede its right to determine national policy on matters of war and peace or its power to require that all citizens assist in the national defense according to their capacity. In effect, government and citizenry say to conscientious objectors whether selective or universal: "We respect your judgment with regard to killing in a war that you regard as unjust, but we require that you contribute to the common good. In particular, we do not regard your understandable interest in not being killed as overriding the needs of the common defense. If this is unacceptable to you and if the war seems so clearly unjust that you cannot participate in it in any way, the path of noncompliance and civil disobedience is open to you. This path brings with it the likelihood of criminal penalties and civil disabilities, which our society will impose with reluctance but firmness in order to preserve important social goods." The combination of legal recognition of selective conscientious objection with a requirement of service is not fully in conformity with the first-order moral judgments of either side about the morality of the actions under consideration, but is a compromise solution in a conflict situation, a solution which attempts to do justice to the most important values of each side.

The second point we should bear in mind in assessing the fourth reason of the Commission is the indeterminacy of just-war theory. This indeterminacy often leads to a suspicion of the motives of those who apply the theory to particular cases and reach conclusions opposite to our own; but it should instead lead us to the expectation that conscientious people applying the norms of the theory will, in hard cases, reach contradictory conclusions. Many wars and uses of force will not be judged in the same way by conscientious men and women. If just-war theory is an incomplete instrument for our moral assessments of the use of force and if our knowledge of the particular situation is, as it most often is, sadly imperfect, and if our conclusions rest on premises that are less than intellectually compelling, we should anticipate the need to develop an ethic of mutual respect and compromise for the sake of the common good. Wars, as we know, can often be bitterly divisive. The necessity for us to judge their justice is urgent, but our confidence in our conscientious judgments about these matters should be limited, and we should be aware of the recurrent temptation to veil our uncertainties behind the smoke and incense of self-righteousness.

The fifth and last of the Commission's reasons for rejecting selective conscientious objection is one that I have most difficulty in dealing with. It is the claim that such a policy will be "disruptive to the morale and effectiveness of the Armed Forces."[19] Never having served in combat or in the armed services, I cannot judge with any precision the likely social consequences within the military of the legal recognition of selective conscientious objection. The Commission makes the point that the justness or unjustness of a war will have to be determined within the context of the war itself. This is true, but we should be careful to keep distinct the context of the war, the duration of the war itself, and actual combat situations. Some wars cast shadows before themselves; and anticipatory judgments about the morality of participating in them can and should be made, though we have to reckon with the possibility and even the likelihood that these judgments will be overturned. I do not think that actual combat situations provide an appropriate place for the making of reflective moral judgments about the justice or injustice of a war taken as a whole. They can and do present moral challenges, about whether a particular action is right or wrong; and these challenges have to be met on the spot. But such challenges, for instance, about whether to treat a peasant as a civilian or a guerrilla, arise whether we recognize selective conscientious objection or not. How the moral challenges and dilemmas of combat are to be worked out without damaging the chain of command and without turning soldiers into killing machines and debasing them as moral agents is a very difficult problem for military leadership. A system of selective conscientious objection should be designed so as to make the standard point for decision about the morality of a current or impending war the draftee's point of entry into the service. A war that has begun or that has significantly altered its character during a person's term of service presents more difficult problems. But we should remember that a war on which public opinion in general is significantly divided will probably present serious problems within the military, whether or not there is legal recognition of selective conscientious objection. It is at least possible that a regular system in which people can voice their conscientious doubts to chaplains and commanding officers, receive counseling and be reassigned is likely to produce less harm to military morale and effectiveness than is a system which handles moral difficulties on an ad hoc basis or tries to suppress them. One must recognize that there is need for discretion in handling these matters so that ripples of dissent and non-compliance do not disable units.

However, I disagree with the Commission's line of argument which in effect treats the exercise of moral judgment by soldiers as an unnecessary and dangerous thing. The Commission argues: "Forcing upon the individual the necessity of making that distinction between just and unjust-wars—which would be the practical effect of taking away the Government's obligation of making it for him—could put a burden heretofore unknown on the man in uniform and even on the brink of combat, with results that could well be disastrous to him, to his unit, and to the entire military tradition."[20] The Commission's argument here has two main elements (1) a claim about the likely negative consequences of recognizing selective conscientious objection, a possibility which should be dealt with carefully, and (2) a controversial assigning of moral roles and obligations in such a way that it is the task of the government and the government alone, at least to the exclusion of persons serving in the military, to deliberate about whether a given war is just or unjust. This seems to recommend, if not to require, an abnegation of moral judgment that is incompatible with the norms of the Nuremberg trials, in which the defense of superior orders was held to be insufficient. The argument also shows a failure to appreciate the value of conscientious moral decision, a value which is at the center of our growth as religious and moral persons and which is an integral part of our social development as a free people. Military life and the exigencies of war require obedience to orders; but in a democracy this must be the obedience of free men and women who are concerned both to protect their society and to preserve their moral integrity. That is why, in the beginning, I proposed that we should regard selective conscientious objection not merely as a right but as a good. It is not a good that is easy to achieve either for individuals or for societies. If it is to work well, it requires patience and courage, prudence and a sense of justice on the part of individuals, a mixture of firmness and forbearance, a respect for freedom and a desire to protect the common good on the part of societies. Selective conscientious objection is one instance of the human person using intelligence to determine to the best of his ability the right course of action in a situation where choice is narrow but supremely important, where evils and temptations abound, where one is required to look carefully at the motives of one's heart and at the sufferings and evils one may cause to others. It is a good surrounded and often obscured by evils. And it is a good with a double aspect. On the one hand, when it is correct, it is a negative response to an unjust-war, one of the greatest evils that can afflict human society. On the other hand, it is an expression of the freedom of the human person to choose the good, whether this be to fight or not to fight, to pick the rose of virtuous action from among the thorns of violence and uncertainty. As such an expression, it should be respected and honored not merely by morally concerned citizens but also by our laws.

Notes

1. William James, "The Will to Believe," *Essays on Faith and Morals* (Cleveland: World Publishing, 1962), p. 34.

2. Moliere, *Les Fourberies de Scapin*, Act II, Scene 7.

3. The conception of negative freedom, to use the terminology of Sir Isaiah Berlin, is clearly present in Hobbes, *Leviathan*, Part I, Chapter 14, where liberty is defined as "the absence of external impediments" and is opposed to law.

4. Justice Oliver Wendell Holmes, *Schenck v. United States*, 249 U.S. 47 (1919).

5. Isaiah Berlin, *Two Concepts of Liberty* (Oxford: Clarendon Press, 1958), pp. 7–16.

6. Attributed to Voltaire in S. G. Tallentyre [Evelyn V. Hall], *The Friends of Voltaire (London: J. Murray, 1906), p. 199.*

7. See, for instance, Robert Nozick, "A Framework for Utopia," *Anarchy, State and Utopia* (N.Y.: Basic Books, 1977), ch. 10.

8. National Advisory Commission on Selective Service, *In Pursuit of Equity: Who Serves When Not All Serve?* (Washington, D.C.: U.S. Government Printing Office, 1967).

9. "Gaudium et Spes," *The Documents of Vatican II,* Walter Abbott and Joseph Gallagher, eds. (N.Y.: America Press, 1966), Para. 79.

10. Ibid. Para. 78.

11. Ibid. Para. 82.

12. *In Pursuit of Equity*, p. 48.

13. Ibid., p. 50.

14. Ibid.

15. Ibid.

16. Ibid.

17. Ibid.

18. Ibid.

19. Ibid.

20. Ibid., p. 51.

8

Alternative Service:
The Significance of the Challenge

James L. Lacy

I address a subject that at first glance might seem to be outside the major theme of this book—which debates an enormously difficult and recurring issue in American public policy. At the risk of oversimplification, that issue pivots on a single set of questions: Whom should the government recognize as conscientious objectors, in what circumstances, and on the basis of what beliefs? I will touch on these questions, but I will address them from a different direction than the other authors. I will suggest that, as a matter of practical public policy, we already have several possible answers, and that none is particularly attractive or palatable. I will focus, instead, on a different, but very much related, dimension.

This second dimension poses a different question: What, if anything, should government require of conscientious objectors, once they have been recognized as such? I refer specifically to alternative, nonmilitary service. I hope to show not only that the two sets of questions are intricately linked, but also that answers to the second—now more than ever before—are crucial in any effort to rationalize public policy in this area. These answers are not to be found easily, and are not to

The views expressed in this paper are wholly those of the author and do not necessarily represent the views of the RAND Corporation or any of its government or corporate sponsors.

be found in past policies or experiences. I will not provide a blueprint, but I will describe the nature and significance of the challenge.

Frames of Reference

Let me begin by specifying the frames of reference. First, by "alternative service," I mean government-recognized-and-sanctioned nonmilitary service, not under military direction, performed in lieu of military service by citizens who otherwise are legally obligated to serve in the military. It is an alternative that has been available as a matter of law since 1940. Although there were proposals in the 1960s to make the option available to others, it has been limited to conscientious objectors. The objector who convinced the government that his conscience, and not his convenience, made military service repugnant had a latitude granted to him alone: he had a nonmilitary alternative to the draft if he wanted it; the discretion not to serve in the armed forces.

This leads to a second point. Alternative service is, in short, a draft alternative. In the case of the present all-volunteer force, the individual is free to reject personal service in the armed forces (at least up to the time he voluntarily enters an enlistment contract); to do so for reasons he need not articulate or defend; and to do so in pursuit of the noblest or basest of intentions. For alternative service—and, indeed, for the full sweep of conscientious objection—to come into play, there must pre-exist the legal obligation to serve, an obligation that, for all practical purposes, does not exist now.

Why, then, discuss a draft alternative in the absence of an immediate draft? There are two reasons.

First, there are many (including quite a few members of Congress) who believe that a resumption of conscription is either desirable or inevitable within the next ten years. They point to the increasing costs of fielding an all-volunteer force, and the fact that our 18-year-old population is steadily diminishing in size—the latter, the result of low birth rates in the 1960s and 1970s. Some are concerned that we have created too great an imbalance between two cherished values: citizen obligation and individual freedom.

Second, the public policy issue attending a resumption of conscription raises the two questions I alluded to earlier: who will be recognized as conscientious objectors, and what will we do with them? As I will show, the case law has virtually paralyzed public policy in this area. We can no longer answer rationally the first question—who?—except by reference to answers to the second—doing what?

In short, I consider a subject that has an abundant and controversial past, no present, but not unreasonable prospects of having a real and enormously difficult future. Let me turn first to the past, and then address the future.

The Heritage

We have a rich, if somewhat erratic, heritage regarding conscientious objection in the United States. It is a long-standing principle of American law that some allowance be made for men who are religiously or conscientiously opposed to the bearing of arms and the killing of other men. America's draft laws have honored individual choice in instances in which conscription and conscience collide, but only in some such instances. The militia drafts excused conscientious objectors from service; the federal draft of 1863 provided them (as well as others) the option to substitute another or pay a commutation fee; the special CO allowance was preserved in all subsequent drafts as well. The individual could be excused from combat, and, after 1940, from military service as well—but only if his judgment was derived from a moral imperative. Not all moral dictates were acceptable. The objector had to object to the right things, for the "right" reasons, and in a demonstrably "right" fashion. Conscientious objection had not only to be asserted; it had to be demonstrated along lines acceptable to the government as well.

This special allowance is not of constitutional dimensions. James Madison's proposal to make conscientious objection a matter of fundamental and enduring protection was explicitly rejected by the Constitutional Convention of 1789. The "right" to special treatment within the terms of a draft is a "right" granted by the grace of the Congress. Supreme Court Justice Harlan made the point in 1970: "Congress, of course, could entirely, consistently with the requirements of the Constitution, eliminate all exemptions for conscientious objectors."[1]

The CO's special status has been available in time of war and in time of peace, regardless of whether the prospect of engaging in actual combat is real, remote or non-existent. Historically, however, the CO's moral opposition has had to be categorical. Moral convictions less capable of absolutist articulation have found no relief in the exception. The Marshall Commission in 1967 expressed the rationale for that view: "Legal recognition of selective pacifism could open the doors to a general theory of selective disobedience to law, which could quickly tear down the fabric of government. The distinction is dim between a person conscientiously opposed to participation in a particular war and one conscientiously opposed to payment of a particular tax."[2]

Along these lines, the CO exception has been limited in the terms by which one can lawfully object: it has been lawful not to don the uniform; it has been unlawful not to pay taxes because they support a particular military policy.[3]

Until the mid-1960s, the special allowance had always been grounded in religion and awarded on the basis of religious distinctions—a form of selection not comfortably squared with the free exercise and establishment clauses of the First Amendment. Before 1940, in fact, the excusal was granted only to members of certain religious congregations. The Confederate draft exempted Friends, Dunkards, Nazarenes and Mennonites; the Union draft, members of religious denominations "conscientiously opposed to the bearing of arms who are prohibited from doing so by the rules and articles of faith and practice." The 1917 draft exempted registrants who were members of a well-recognized religious sect whose creed forbade personal participation in combat in any form. Such distinctions did not trouble the Supreme Court at the time. It pronounced constitutional the World War I CO provisions in 1918, declaring the answer so obvious it required neither explanation nor discussion.[4]

In 1940, the Congress broadened the excusal to include objectors regardless of congregational affiliation, but it still insisted that there be religious content. Philosophical, sociological and political convictions, no matter how deeply held, were insufficient. This, however, only made for other difficult questions. What had to be religious: the person or his views? How, absent reference to the theology or recognized precepts of an organized religion, was one to judge whether views were religious or nonreligious? What, indeed, was religion?

After 1918, the Supreme Court, for the most part, was silent. When it finally did speak, it did so opaquely. The obvious Constitutional question, which had not troubled the Court in 1918, concerned distinctions made on the basis of religious beliefs. The Court of the 1960s and 1970s, however, showed no disposition to take that question on. Assiduously avoiding constitutional questions, the Court turned to statutory interpretation, in the process construing the intentions of Congress and the words of the statute in ways that made both unrecognizable and unintelligible. In the *Seeger* case in 1965, the Court redefined "religion" to include atheistic views, provided these views were possessed with a fervor similar to that of subscribers to more orthodox religions. The new test, in the Court's words, was: "A sincere and meaningful belief which occupies in the life of its possessor a place parallel to that filled by the God of those admittedly qualifying for the exemption comes within the statutory definition [of religious belief]."[5]

In 1970, in *Welsh v. United States*,[6] the Court struck another blow for obscurantism. The conscription statute excluded from CO status beliefs that were essentially political, sociological, or philosophical views or a merely personal moral code. "Nevertheless," said the Court, "if an individual deeply and sincerely holds beliefs that are purely ethical or moral in source and content, but that nevertheless impose on him a duty of conscience to refrain from participating in any war at any time, those beliefs certainly occupy in the life of the individual 'a place parallel to that filled by God.' "[7] Welsh did not view his opposition as religious. No matter, said the court. In its words: "The Court's statement in *Seeger* that a registrant's characterization of his own belief as 'religious' should carry great weight does not imply that his declaration that his views are nonreligious should be treated similarly."[8] Welsh, too, was a conscientious objector for purposes of the draft law.

The Supreme Court had avoided the constitutional question, but at considerable cost. From a constitutionally suspicious but reasonably intelligible set of criteria in 1918, the Court had moved the nation to a test so ethereal that it seemed beyond the ability of ordinary people to apply. Who, now, was a conscientious objector and who was not? Atheists qualified, as did persons whose beliefs were not religious, so long as they opposed all wars; persons with religious objections to less than war in any form, did not. And how could one apply these mystical tests in a real-world setting? If a draft registrant said the right words was this enough? How does one measure moral conviction?

The Congress tried, with no success, to rewrite the statute. Selective Service bravely issued new instructions to draft boards—these were about as lucid as the court decision that required them. To an observer like Harvard Law School professor John Mansfield: "It is certainly permissible to wonder whether the authority of Congress is really any more respected by the sort of strenuous statutory interpretation that the Court indulged in to avoid a constitutional question than it would be by an outright holding of unconstitutionality."

Mercifully, the draft ended within two years of the *Welsh* decision. The wandering case law of the Vietnam-era was frozen in time.

I have summarized this part of the past in order to underscore a singularly powerful point. Were the nation to resume compulsory military service, it would promptly return to the same baffling mess. We have lost our ability to legislate in this area in ways that are acceptable both constitutionally and as a matter of public policy. With a resumption of conscription, we would face a terrible dilemma: either a voluntary draft—a contradiction in terms in which you are a CO if you say you are, because we have no acceptable, intelligible means to discriminate—or the need to abolish the CO exemption entirely. Neither is an attractive choice. If we are required to choose only in these terms, I have little doubt about how we will choose as a nation. We will not compromise our national security, and we will not tell young men in dangerous military positions that they are there simply because they are not clever enough not to be there.

Alternative Service

Let me, however, turn to another part of the past, and the main subject of this chapter, in order to develop the linkage. The excusal of COs was not normally unconditional. If only combat offended moral sensibilities, military service in a noncombatant capacity was expected. If military service itself conflicted with conscience, the CO was expected to perform a nonmilitary alternative for a period of equivalent duration.

The 1863 draft law required religious objectors to do one of four things in lieu of military service: find a substitute, pay a commutation fee, work in hospitals, or care for freedmen. Initially, the World War I draft acknowledged only opposition to combat. Objectors could elect noncombatant duty, but those who objected to military service itself faced imprisonment. However, a way was eventually found to furlough many COs out of military duty and into agricultural work and service with the American Friends Reconstruction Units in France.

The 1940 draft added a new provision. Those who opposed military service itself did not have to serve in uniform. Instead, the law provided that they perform assigned work of national importance under civil direction, at approved work camps sponsored by the historic peace churches, other religious groups, and the government. Twelve thousand COs joined these Civilian Public Service camps—most left over from the Civilian Conservation Corps program of the 1930s—to do CCC-like conservation work for the war's duration. Seventy percent stuck it out through demobilization in 1945.

With the resumption of conscription in 1948, the CO exemption was retained. Through apparent inadvertence—and because the World War II camps had been shut down—the requirement for alternative service was dropped. Within three years, however, alternative service was back. The 1951 Act restored "civilian work of importance in the national health, safety or interest" as a condition for conscientious avoidance of military service. Henceforth, however, COs would find qualifying work on their own, or would be placed by the Selective Service System, but at not direct cost to the government. There would be no work camps, and no single work program as such.

These provisions remained unchanged through the Vietnam War. How many men qualified for and performed alternative service, and what precisely they did, are lost to history—at least in terms of the records of the Selective Service System.

We do, however, know something about Vietnam. Vietnam-era COs differed from their World War II counterparts and from the men who were inducted. COs in the Vietnam years were overwhelmingly white, mostly middle class, and with considerably greater education than the men who were inducted. According to a survey conducted by Selective Service in the early 1970s, they had more than 15 years of formal education on average; more than 40 percent were college graduates; more than 70 percent had some college education; and only 4 percent had not completed high school. Very few were black.

Selective Service was sensitive to these patterns, but placed the blame elsewhere. In the words of one of its reports to the Congress: ". . . .The *Welsh* decision merely increases the advantage of the better educated registrants to be classified as a conscientious objector. Thus, any complaint about Selective Service guidelines most appropriately might be lodged against the bias inherent in the concept of conscientious objection."

A postscript by Basker and Strauss, who worked on President Ford's Clemency Board, suggested that alternative service was something less than advertised. "Conscientious objection did not involve considerable hardship," according to their findings. "Almost all of the 172,000 vietnam-era COs were asked to do alternative service in lieu of induction. . . . Many worked as hospital orderlies or as conservation workers." But many performed not all. Harried draft boards often provided little supervision of the program; almost 50,000 COs simply "dropped out" and never performed service; fewer than 1,000 were convicted for refusing to participate. Also, Selective Service fell behind in its placements. By 1971, more than 34,000 COs were awaiting placement in alternative service, many of them having waited for years. Selective Service explained: "The present economy has made the placement of conscientious objectors more difficult."

By the time of All-Volunteer Force, there was little in logic or practice to command the CO exemption. COs, it seemed, were all those who made the correctly-phrased claim, and no others. The system merely and ritualistically applied the intellectually wilted tests concocted by a Supreme Court that had faced an impossible issue and blinked. Alternative service had lost much of its value and most of its credibility. To be sure, there were many earnest COs who performed valuable nonmilitary service. The problem was that the system had no way to distinguish between serious claims and serious people on the one hand, and the not very serious on the other.

The Past and Future

What, then, does these two strands of the past say for the future? I would suggest that if we are to retain any exemption from military service for conscientious objectors, we must acquire a credible means to distinguish between the serious and the frivolous—between opposition based on conscience, and that merely motivated by convenience. Our traditional means of doing this—what may be called the belief test—makes little sense after the *Welsh* decision. It might still be employed to weed out "incorrect" CO claims from "correct" petitions, but that is a bookkeeping measure, not to be confused with a sound, sensible or defensible public policy. Besides, inquiring into the moral beliefs of individuals is always a dubious and unattractive proposition. The less we do of it, the better.

The only real alternative, apart from abolishing the exemption entirely, is to focus on the other side of the equation. In requiring alternative service in the past, we have been animated by two considerations. The first is a notion of equity: in fairness to the person inducted into the military, the person excused should be required to perform one service to his countrymen of at least equivalent duration, if not equivalent hardship. The second consideration is, in fact, an effort to distinguish. Those who, at least, will perform alternative service are to be taken more seriously than those who would attempt to opt out entirely. Put another way, the existence of the requirement for alternative service has been seen as a means to discourage frivolous claims.

Yet, if we are to deemphasize belief tests—as I believe we have to, should and must—and emphasize instead the obligation to serve in a nonmilitary capacity, an entirely new approach to alternative service will be required. The World War II work camps were farcical: too many COs, and not enough useful work. The program of the 1950s and 1960s—and especially during Vietnam—was hardly a matter of equity, and scarcely a program at all. We would be better off doing nothing with COs, or abolishing the CO exception entirely, than trivializing the process with half-baked and half-hearted measures.

In 1939, the American Friends Service Committee sponsored a project in upstate New York intending to demonstrate to the Roosevelt Administration that COs would serve in a productive nonmilitary capacity should war come. The project was a volunteer camp in which pacifists of both sexes worked for six months to a year without pay in the forestation program of the Oswego County Farmers' Cooperative.

I mention this, not to suggest that something like it be done again, but rather, to make a broader point. For government and the religious communities—and especially for the religious communities—the challenge ahead will be to establish serious, credible alternative service outlets for COs; for the individual, the obligation will be to perform that service. That challenge is imposing. As a nation, we are not particularly adept at creating useful work programs—particularly when we impose a legal requirement for certain persons to work in these programs.

Yet, without serious, concentrated planning for such a program, I doubt we can, as a nation, return to a draft and excuse no one who is obligated to serve. Without serious and serious-minded advance planning, and help from those most immediately concerned with how we reconcile the conscience with the calls of citizenship, I doubt that we will choose wisely.

This, then, is the challenge I pose. I will not provide the details of such a program—what size, what kind of work, how long, how compensated. For one thing, I do not possess the technical talents to do so. For another thing, more importantly, this is no simple matter. Each dimension of such a program is a presentation in itself, and each entails a bouquet of controversies and considerations.

I can imagine a point in time when we no longer examine the moral beliefs of those who oppose military service—not only because such is inherently unmanageable and distasteful in a free society, but also because we will then know that those who do not serve, will serve, and will serve in a valuable and credible manner in nonmilitary capacities. We probably will not be there anytime soon.

But to get there—indeed, to get any place—will require that we take a page from William James' 1910 essay: "A Moral Equivalent of War." Noting what he called "certain deficiencies in the program of pacifism," James argued that a peaceful economy cannot be a "simple pleasure economy." For James, the answer was to conscript an "Army enlisted against Nature" to do imposing and severe work in the national interest, so that "they would tread the earth more proudly." In other words, not to merely opt out, but to rigorously and convincingly demonstrate to society that a man of particular conscience, whatever the character of his beliefs, can and will serve his country, as well as his conscience, in serious and significant fashion.

The specifics of James' proposal have little applicability to a much different world 80 years later, but the concept endures. It requires that this generation take the time and care to see it through—to imagine bold and difficult ideas, and to persuade ourselves, and others, in and out of government, that there is a real alternative, and that we are prepared and capable to make a sparkling and significant reality of it.

Notes

1. *Welsh v. United States*, 398 U.S. 358 (1970).
2. National Advisory Commission on Selective Service, *In Pursuit of Equity: Who Serves When Not all Serve?* (Washington: USGPO, 1967).
3. *United States v. Lee*, 455 U.S. 25 (1982).
4. *The Selective Draft Cases*, 245 U.S. 366 (1918).
5. *United States v. Seeger*, 380 U.S. 163, 176 (1965).
6. 398 U.S. 333 (1970).
7. Ibid. at 343–44.
8. Ibid.

9

In-Service Conscientious Objection

Edward F. Sherman

The discharge of service members who became conscientious objectors after induction is a logical extension of our national policy of "exempting from military service those whose consciences will not permit them to bear arms for their country."[1] "Respect for the value of conscientious action and for the principle of supremacy of conscience" and the pragmatic recognition of "the hopelessness of converting a sincere conscientious objector into an effective fighting man"[2] justify applying the same standards to CO's whether their views crystalized before or after induction. It was not until 1962, however, that the Department of Defense issued regulations providing for the discharge of in-service conscientious objectors.[3] Although the DOD directive relies on the same substantive standards for CO status as the Selective Service Act, its implementation raises distinctive problems for the in-service conscientious objector.

The present Department of Defense directive emphasizes that CO discharge "is discretionary with the military service concerned," must be "consistent with the effectiveness and efficiency of the military services," and will only be granted "to the extent practicable and equitable."[4] These caveats seem inconsistent with the tracking of the Selective Service Act's substantive standards, which rest on the principle that respect for conscience overrides governmental and military concerns about manpower needs. Indeed, some attempts by the military services to deviate from expansive court interpretation of Selective Service substantive standards (for example, the *Seeger* extension of coverage to non-religious CO's) have not been upheld by the courts.[5] The DOD directive's grudging attitude towards CO discharge, however, has been reflected in the manner in which discharge applications are processed and determined.

The In-Service CO Process

The DOD directive sets out detailed procedures for processing CO applications. The applicant is interviewed by a chaplain and military psychiatrist, and an investigating officer outside the chain of command conducts an informal hearing at which the applicant may submit evidence. The investigating officer then forwards the record, together with his recommendation, to the commanding officer, who adds his recommendation and forwards it through the chain of command to the headquarters of the service. The process is cumbersome and time-consuming, no doubt accounting in part for the fact that throughout the Vietnam era there were only 17,000 in-service CO applications.[6]

The criteria for CO status set out in the directive require a demonstration that: (1) the applicant is conscientiously opposed to participation in war in any form; (2) the opposition is founded on religious training and beliefs (or moral and ethical convictions "of equal strength, depth and duration" as traditional religious convictions); and (3) the position is sincere and deeply held.[7] The directive generally tracks Selective Service case law, although it sometimes uses language suggesting stricter requirements or special military considerations. For example, it says the burden is on the applicant to prove the claim to CO status "by clear and convincing evidence." Courts, however, have generally ignored this standard,[8] finding that an applicant establishes a prime facie case by making "nonfrivolous allegations that, if true, would be sufficient under regulation or statute to warrant granting the requested classification."[9]

As in Selective Service processing of CO applications, the central question as to the nature and sincerity of the applicant's beliefs requires a judgment on the subjective matter of intent. The nature of the fact-finder then becomes critical. The movement during the Vietnam War to add younger draft board members with more diverse backgrounds attests to the policy concern that for decisions affecting who will serve in the military to be accepted by society, decision-makers should represent a cross-section of society. The in-service CO process, of course, relies entirely on military officers, and thus poses at least initial concerns as to its objectivity.

The DOD process reasonably tries to fashion an objective record from which the nature and sincerity of beliefs can be determined and later reviewed. Inevitably an applicant who has had the benefit of advice from a lawyer or one familiar with the CO process is at a distinct advantage. The directive reflects concern over this possibility, adding admonitory language, for example, that "care must be exercised in determining the integrity of belief and the consistency of application" and that "information presented by the claimant should be sufficient to convince that the claimant's personal history reveals views and actions strong enough to demonstrate that expediency or avoidance of military service is not the basis of his claim."[10]

Some military officials view the process as inadequate to protect military interests. An Air Force Major, concerned over the impact of federal court decisions on military mobilization, has warned that "many officers and enlisted men are capable, with proper counseling and guidance, of putting together a CO application that will pass muster" under what he considers to be unduly lax court decisions.[11] Investigating officers, he says, "are frequently ill-prepared to cope with petitioner's counsel and experience great difficulty in gauging the applicant's sincerity" and lack the resources to conduct "anything analogous to an FBI inquiry."[12] These are legitimate concerns, but the trick is to insure a process whereby CO applications are carefully scrutinized to insure against manufactured claims while not preconditioning the administering officers (who, by the very nature of their profession, are often unsympathetic to conscientious objection) to hostility and inflexible skepticism. A continuing problem in the in-service CO process is how to monitor the recommendations and decisions of the administering officers to insure that their personal views, or what they consider to be the interests of the service, are not substituted for legally-established standards.

Vietnam Era Experience with CO Discharges

The Vietnam era provides a troubling example of abuse of discretion by military administrators in the CO discharge process in the perceived interests of protecting manpower levels and military efficiency. Expanded judicial review ultimately provided a corrective for the worst abuses, but subtle forms of abuse of discretion can still arise which are even more difficult to detect through monitoring and judicial review.

Shortly after the beginning of the American troop buildup in Vietnam in 1965, there was a dramatic decrease in approval rates on CO applications. In the two years before 1965, almost 50 percent of the applicants for CO status from the Army were found to be sincere. In 1965, the percentage slipped to 25 percent, and then, dramatically, to 5 percent in 1966 and 1967. By 1968, the Central Committee for Conscientious Objectors advised in its handbook that "although many men were discharged on grounds of conscience previous to the spring of 1966, since that time almost all discharges have been denied regardless of merit."[13]

The change in approval rates can be explained in part by an increase in nonmeritorious CO applications in the wake of new draft calls for a "shooting" war. But the people who worked with conscientious objectors (such as traditional pacifist groups, religions, and legal assistance organizations) found that the strength of the case made little difference, the services simply were not granting most CO applications. The new hostility was particularly manifested in commanders' recommendations, with chaplains and psychiatrists often more neutral in their evaluations (although their attitudes varied considerably with such personal characteristics as age and career-status). An overriding consideration for many military officials involved in CO processing seemed to be concern over the threat it posed to manpower needs for Vietnam and morale within their units. As a result, there were many cases in which the wrong legal standard was applied (for example, denials based on finding that an applicant was not a pacifist, was not a member of a traditional pacifist religion, or was not motivated by orthodox religious beliefs). In other cases, CO status was denied although there was nothing in the record to provide any basis in fact for not believing the applicant and the evidence he presented.

The costs of this arbitrariness were high. A study of the deserters who returned under the Ford Amnesty Program in 1974 shows that some deserted only after being denied proper consideration of their CO applications.[14] In federal court cases in Indiana (where the Amnesty Program was located), a number of amnesty program participants were ordered to be honorably discharged because of the military's failure to have properly considered their CO applications.[15]

There was little legal recourse for the unsuccessful applicant early in the Vietnam War era. A long line of federal court decisions had established the "nonreviewability" of military determinations concerning its own personnel. Premised on the sensible-enough dictum that "judges are not given the task of running the Army,"[16] this doctrine prevented federal courts from considering, either on writs of habeas corpus or mandamus, challenges to even the most lawless denials of CO discharge.

Judicial Review

The unavailability of civilian court review was finally altered in 1968 when a United States Circuit Court of Appeals, in the landmark decision of *Hammond v. Lenfest*, [17] ruled that federal courts could review the military's refusal to grant a conscientious objector discharge without making the serviceman go through a court-martial first. Hammond was a naval reservist who had joined the reserves four years before at the age of seventeen but had since become a member of the Society of Friends and claimed to be a conscientious objector. His request for discharge was denied, and when he failed to attend reserve drills, he was ordered to report for active duty. He sought a writ of habeas corpus, claiming that there was no "basis in fact" for the military's finding that he was not a sincere CO, thus invoking a ground which had already been permitted for judicial review of draft board decisions refusing to grant conscientious objector status.

The "basis in fact" test had two separate aspects. The first was that if the denial of CO status *may* have rested on an illegal ground or an erroneous concept of the law, it must be reversed as having no basis in fact.[18] The second arose if the denial contained no evidentiary facts compatible with the applicant's proof of conscientious objector status.[19]

A corollary of the "basis in fact" test was that reasons must be given and evidence cited for an administrator's decision. This is an important check on administrator arbitrariness. If a court on judicial review did no more than search the record to see if there was some support for the ruling, administrators would be encouraged to shot-gun the record in hopes that the court might be persuaded by some reason, whether or not it was really the basis for the decision. This would rob the applicant of his right to have a responsible official decide on the basis of clearly defined reasons and would force the court to perform the administrator's proper function.[20]

The *Hammond* court determined that the military's refusal to discharge him as a conscientious objector was subject to limited judicial review to determine if there was a "basis in fact." It also found that he had not failed to exhaust his military remedies, that is, that he need not have refused to perform military service and gone through a court-martial in order to obtain court review. Refusing to intermingle nonreviewability with the exhaustion issue, it found that the objectives of exhaustion would not be met by demanding submittal to court-martial. The highest authority in the military's administrative scheme had already made a negative determination, Hammond had no power to convene a court-martial, and even if one were convened, there was no indication "that presenting a conscientious objector claim as a defense to a charge of violating military law by failing to obey orders would be anything more than a futile and ritualistic gesture."[21]

Within a year, four other Federal Circuit Courts of Appeal (out of a total of ten) took the same position.[22] The *Hammond* decision had a tremendous impact on the military's handling of conscientious objector discharges. Suddenly, the military was no longer immune from civilian court review, and the officers who administered CO discharges were faced with the unpleasant prospect of having their refusals overturned in federal courts because they had applied the wrong legal standard or had "no basis in fact" for their findings. As the number of suits seeking to overturn the military's refusal to discharge steadily increased, the military beat a hasty retreat. By 1970 the percentage of favorable decisions was back up to the rate of approximately 50 percent that had prevailed before 1965.

The services did have to commit more personnel to processing applications, some of them groundless, and military lawyers had to spend more time responding to habeas corpus petitions. But from hindsight, predictions that a portion of the armed forces would be rendered immobile and entangled in litigation were off the mark. Military autonomy was affected in the sense that commanding officers, chaplains, psychiatrists, and other military officials involved in processing discharge applications had to be more careful to insure that they followed regulations and to give reasons and documentation for any denial. But, like police and other governmental officials who sometimes chafe over the exactitude required of them by court-enforced standards of due process, they came to accept more legalistic standards as part of the routine processing of discharge applications. Today the standards for "basis in fact" review are contained in the DOD directive, and military administrators are aware that the courts may be looking over their shoulders.

Status Pending Processing of CO Application

In-service conscientious objection poses one problem not present in selective service—what to do with the individual pending processing of his application for CO discharge. The applicant remains in the military and is subject to military orders and law, but, as a professed CO, he maintains that any formal participation in support of the military is contrary to his conscience. Ideally he might be sent home to await the determination and, in a few cases of officers, this has been done. But the services are understandably unwilling to relinquish control, and the regulations provide that "applicants will be expected to conform to the normal requirements of military service and to perform satisfactorily such duties to which they are assigned."[23] The only concession to conscience is the provision that "to the extent practicable under the circumstances . . . every effort will be made to assign applicants to duties within the command to which they are assigned which will conflict as little as possible with their asserted beliefs."[24]

During the early part of the Vietnam War, regulations provided that CO applicants would be processed at the installation where they made application. This led to attempts to avoid being sent to Vietnam by filling CO applications just before shipment. In 1970, the Pacific Counseling Service conducted a leafleting campaign of soldiers passing through the Oakland Army Base bound for Vietnam, and some twelve hundred troops applied for CO status within a few weeks.[25] The regulations were quickly changed to prohibit applying for CO status en route to Vietnam. The regulations now provide that individuals on reassignment orders may be required to submit CO applications at their next permanent duty station.[26] The services maintain that sending professed COs into a battle zone (or onto a battle-ready nuclear submarine in the Navy) is not inconsistent with the obligation to assign duties that will conflict as little as possible with the applicant's beliefs.

Defense of Unlawful Orders
to Court Martial for Disobedience

A CO applicant may raise the defense of unlawful orders if he is court-martialled for disobedience of orders to which he should not have been assigned. A 1972 Air Force Board of Review decision involving three airmen known as "the Phu Cat 3" demonstrates the complexity of the issues surrounding CO applications made in battlefield situations.[27] Three airmen who were security policemen in the sentry dog section at Phu Cat Air Base in Vietnam decided, after much talking among themselves, that they were CO's. One testified at their court-martial:

> So we went up there [to see the Captain] and he said "Why aren't you prepared to go on post"? We told him that we didn't feel we should go on post anymore, this whole war, this war was against what we believed and were going to have to make our stand finally, and he told us, "I am giving you a direct order to report for duty tonight and to go on post with the others," and I told him I would go on post, do everything I could, but I would not carry a weapon in the K-9 section or anywhere else anymore.[28]

They were convicted by court-martial of refusal of orders and sentenced to dishonorable discharges and confinement at hard labor for six months. They claimed, on appeal, that they were entitled to be assigned to duties consistent with their beliefs. The Board of Review found that the military judge had incorrectly instructed the court that the airmen were not entitled to the benefits of the regulation. It found that, despite the need for combat readiness, there was sufficient evidence to raise an issue as to the practicability of their not carrying weapons (indeed, they were allowed to perform guard duties for four nights without weapons) and therefore their entitlement to the protections of the regulation. The Board also found that the airmen were entitled to the protection of the regulation even though they had not formally applied for CO status since they clearly made their desire to apply known to their commanding officer.

The defense of unlawful orders may also apply to a service member who refuses to perform military duties after he is wrongfully denied CO status. In *United States v. Sigmon*,[29] the defendant was court-martialled for disobeying an order to enplane for Vietnam, issued after the military authorities had refused to process his CO claim for discharge. The Army Board of Review ruled that the order, while lawful on its face, became illegal by the failure to consider the application. In creating a new precedent contrary to related rulings on the subject, the tribunal spoke in broad terms:

> While we are aware of no specific case in point, we are of the view that an order, even though lawful on its face, that has its foundation in an unlawful act of the government is tainted by the act and is also unlawful. Stated somewhat more positively, appellant should have been permitted to execute and file the required form and had he done so, he would never have been placed in the position that he has found himself ever since he was given the order. As the order was illegal, appellant could not have missed the movement through design.[30]

The U.S. Court of Military Appeals narrowed the potentially expansive scope of *Sigmon* in *U.S. v. Noyd*.[31] This case involved an Air Force Captain who refused an order to train jet pilots, issued after his CO application had been turned down.

Captain Noyd claimed that he could not carry out this assignment without contradicting his deeply held beliefs. His commanding officer had purposely waited until the application had been denied before giving the order, so that the duty limitations required by Air Force regulations would no longer have effect. In this situation the Court of Military Appeals ruled that the validity of the commander's order turned on the validity of the Secretary's decision to deny the application. "If the Secretary's decision was illegal, the order it generated was illegal."[32] If the Secretary had improperly denied Noyd the status of a conscientious objector, the commanding officer had no authority to require him to train pilots. The court thus assumed, without actually deciding, that the duties in question conflicted with his CO belief. The Secretary's determination, however was found to be correct, because Noyd objected only to the Vietnam War and not to all wars. Thus he had no right to be exempted from combatant duties.

Implicit in *Noyd* was the proposition that orders not inconsistent with the beliefs of a conscientious objector are valid, even when a CO application has been wrongfully denied. The Court of Military Appeals considerably expanded this position in *Jones v. Lemond*[33] in finding that a service member may not assert conscientious objection as a defense to charges of AWOL. It did not matter if the military had wrongfully refused to process the CO application or had denied it without basis in fact. Nor did it matter if the purpose of the AWOL was to seek the assistance of legal counsel in an attempt to challenge the military's action. In the court's view, a service member simply has no justification for absenting himself from duty whether a CO application were pending or not.

In applying the *Lemond* decision, military tribunals have maintained that certain orders are inherently lawful because their validity exists independently of any pending CO application. By definition, inherently lawful orders do not impose more than minimum conflict with asserted beliefs and therefore conform to the requirements of the regulation. Thus, a CO applicant cannot refuse orders to wear the uniform, get a haircut, attend lectures, or perform routine maintenance duties. He cannot be required to handle weapons, but can be ordered to perform functions that support military operations. This, of course, ignores the fact that a sincere CO cannot conscientiously participate in even the most mundane duties that further the war aims of the armed forces.

Insensitivity to this moral position has led to the conclusion that CO applicants can be required to engage in riot control training. The Army Court of Military Review reasoned that a person conscientiously opposed to war would not be opposed to "para-police duties," as long as he participated without arms.[34] But a sincere CO would likely refuse such an assignment because civil disturbance troops most often use violence, sometimes lethal in nature. The Court's analysis indicates the extent to which military tribunals have misunderstood the premises of conscientious objection when considering the scope of duty assignments. By equating objection to war with objection to bearing arms, the military has forced CO applicants to assert their beliefs at the risk of criminal punishment.

Processing of ROTC Applicants for CO Discharge

Applications for CO discharge by ROTC cadets who have taken the oath of induction is not an uncommon event. The usual practice in the services was for such applications to be processed while the cadet continued in school (assuming application was made in sufficient time before graduation). Like other CO applicants, the cadet would be entitled under service regulations to be assigned duties not inconsistent with his or her beliefs. In 1983, the Air Force issued new regulations that provide that an ROTC applicant for CO discharge must first go through a disenrollment process for "anticipatory breach" of the ROTC contract and then apply for CO discharge from the Air Force Reserve.[35] This means that the cadet could be disenrolled and then called to active duty before his claim is processed and determined by the reserves.[36] It ignores the fact that a cadet who invokes the CO discharge process is simply asserting rights granted under military regulations and that such invocation should not be considered tantamount to breach of contract.

The Air Force disenrollment process means that ROTC applications are determined by active duty Air Force officers, rather than by the ROTC personnel who are most familiar with the individual involved. It also forces the cadet to undergo two separation processes, with separate hearings and additional pressure and time. This is a harsh rule, apparently aimed at discouraging CO applications by ROTC cadets. The punitive intent seems to outweigh any legitimate military purpose.

Conclusion

Vietnam War litigation brought needed regularity to the CO application process. But problems of unfairness can still result from the grudging attitude of the regulations, the all-officer nature of the administrators, the degree of discretion they exercise, and the uncertainty of status pending determination of an application. The picture is much improved since the Vietnam War, but there is still reason for concern that rights of conscience are not adequately protected.

Notes

1.	*Gee v. United States*, 319 F.Supp. 581, 582 (S.D.Tex. 1970).
2.	*Gillette v. United States*, 401 U.S. 437, 447 (1971).
3.	DOD Directive 1200.6 [now replaced by 32 CFR § 75.1-75.11 (7/1/86 ed.)]. Some services, however, had previously informally granted discharges for conscientious objection.

4. 32 CFR § 75.4(a).

5. L. Baskir & W. Strauss, *Chance and Circumstance: The Draft, The War and The Vietnam Generation* (N.Y.: Vintage, 1978).

6. Ibid.

7. 32 CFR § 75.5(a).

8. *Selinger v. Claytor*, No. 78-712 (D. Mass. 1978).

9. *Sanger v. Seamans*, 507 F.2d 814 (9th Cir. 1974), quoting *Mulloy v. United States*, 398 U.S. 410 (1970).

10. 32 CFR § 75.5(c)(2).

11. Bruinooge, "Mobilization for a European War: The Impact of Habeas Corpus," *Air Force L. Rev.* (1980–1981)22: 205 at 230.

12. *Ibid.* p. 231.

13. Central Committee for Conscientious Objectors, *Handbook for Conscientious Objectors* (Philadelphia, 10th ed. 1968) 91.

14. *Chance and Circumstance*, 95, 140–42, 184.

15. *Pither v. Schlesinger*, No. IP 75-28-C (S.D. Ind.); *Beish v. Schlesinger*, No. IP 75-39-C (S.D. Ind.); *Eischen v. Schlesinger*, No. IP 75-39-C (S.D. Ind.); *Norr v. Schlesinger*, No. IP 75-131-C (S.D. Ind.), 3 Mil. L. R. 2256.

16. *Orloff v. Willoughby*, 345 U.S. 83, 93 (1953).

17. 398 F.2d 705 (2d Cir. 1968). See discussion in Sherman, "Judicial Review of Military Determinations and the Exhaustion of Remedies Requirement," *Va. L. Rev.* (1969) 55: 483, 514–26.

18. *Sicurella v. United States*, 348 U.S. 385 (1955); *United States v. Lemmens*, 430 F.2d 619 (7th Cir. 1970); *United States v. French*, 429 F.2d 391 (9th Cir. 1970).

19. *Witmer v. United States*, 348 U.S. 375 (1954); *Dickinson v. United States*, 346 U.S. 389 (1953).

20. See *Joseph v. United States*, 405 U.S. 1006 (1972).

21. 398 F.2d at 713.

22. *In re Kelly*, 401 F.2d 211 (5th Cir. 1968); *United States ex rel. Brooks v. Clifford*, 409 F.2d 700, pet. for rehearing denied, 412 F.2d 1137 (4th Cir. 1969); *Bates v. Commander*, 413 F.2d 475 (1st Cir. 1969); *United States ex rel. Sheldon v. O'Malley*, 420 F.2d 1344 (D.C. Cir. 1969).

23. 32 CFR § 75.6(h).

24. Ibid.

25. *Chance and Circumstance*, 58.

26. 32 CFR § 75.6(h).

27. *United States v. Wells*, 45 C.M.R. 501 (ACMR 1972).

28. Ibid., 509–10.

29. 1 S.S.L.R. 3054 (ABR 1968).

30. Ibid., 3055.

31. 18 U.S.C.M.A. 483, 40 C.M.R. 195 (1969).

32. Ibid., 492, 40 C.M.R. at 204.

33. 18 U.S.C.M.A. 513, 40 C.M.R. 225 (1969).

34. *United States v. Chase*, 43 C.M.R. 693 (ACMR 1971).

35. Air Force Reg. 45–10 (1 Aug. 1983).

36. See "New Air Force ROTC Disenrollment Process," *The Objector* (Mar. 1984), pp. 10–11.

10

The Moral Judgment, Action, and Credibility of Israeli Soldiers Who Refused to Serve in Lebanon (1982–1985)

Ruth Linn

Moral Judgment and Action in Real Life Practice

All that the Lord hath spoken we will DO and HEAR.

—Exodus 24:7

This unquestioning acceptance of the Ten Commandments by the people of Israel portrays the moral person as the one whose actions are guided by certain external standards of excellence. By preceding HEAR with DO, the people of Israel did not simply conform to a set of rules but indicated their willingness to transform "religious laws into personal commands of a personal deity."[1] But did they, indeed, succeed in pursuing this goal? In spite of their dramatic promise, the people of Israel found that in real life practice, it is not easy to follow hypothetically prescribed moral principles. Moses climbed to Mount Sinai but did not return for forty days. When they were left alone without their leader, when the situation was ambiguous and all their familiar expectations collapsed, and while still holding the habitual state of mind as slaves, their first action under the pressure of circumstances was an immoral one—the building of another god, the Golden Calf.

In light of this discrepancy between the manifestation of hypothetical (verbal) prediction of moral competence and its actual practice, the dramatic placement of the action (DO) prior to the judgment (HEAR) is indeed quite puzzling. It was also a puzzle for biblical interpreters who questioned the psychological dynamic of the construction of another god in light of the unique moral commitment to one god. The interpreters argued that in real life practice the moral decision maker is always heavily dependent upon contextual forces, mainly that of time (historical time), place (contextual influences) and habit (dominant personal tendencies). Personal

129

freedom in judgment and action, they further suggested, might be obtained only in the case of total devotion to the Torah.

Following the inquiry for the source of personal wisdom used by an individual in conflicting moral situations, the New Testament shifted the emphasis from external criteria to "intrinsically valuable" criteria held by the human being who "will develop his potential worth" if given the opportunity.[2] This concept of the individual as free actor, essentially capable of rising above the circumstances of his environment by his own virtue, represents a different ideological position: the view of the moral person as having free choice and freedom to affect his own salvation.[3] Historically, this view became central to the doctrine of modern education up to Dewey and is now expressed in Lawrence Kohlberg's theory of, and research on, moral development.

Kohlberg[4] conceptualized six age-related stages of moral reasoning which develop over time and experience, and represent a gradual increase of the internal moral capacity to the point where the person's judgment is freed from individual and societal constraints. It entails the premise that the morally mature person will become autonomous in his functioning.

Kohlberg groups the six moral stages into three major levels or perspectives with respect to society's moral norms: preconventional, conventional and postconventional perspectives:

Preconventional: this perspective emerges from an egocentric point of view and characterizes children's moral logic. Stage 1 represents an unreflective acceptance of rules and labels while the command itself is never challenged. Stage 2 represents those judgments which recognize a possible conflict between a rule and individual needs.

Conventional: this perspective, used by most adults, encompasses an understanding of the origin and the function of rules as social utilities. Stage 3 judgment reflects awareness of mutual interpersonal expectations, relationships, and conformity. In Stage 4, the individual reaches the abstract: she/he realizes the role of the rules in the preservation of the society at large yet realizes that under specific circumstances disobeying the law fosters maintenance of the social system.

Postconventional: this perspective (which is also called the principled level) is used by that minority of individuals within society who succeed in obtaining and holding an objective, and even impartial, point of view on a morally controversial situation. Stage 5 embodies a social contract view of the relationship between individuals and society based on utilitarian considerations. Stage 6 (which does not exist in practice) is based on respect for the dignity of individuals as ends, and of morality as justice. Postconventional or principled thinking entails the premise that when there is a conflict between the legal and the moral domains, the moral should almost always take precedence because it represents the more objective and impartial solution within and across societies.

Utilizing Kohlberg's theoretical framework, I have attempted to describe the moral judgment and action of thirty-six Israeli reserve soldiers who refused to serve in Lebanon when called on to perform service there. The description will follow three stages of analysis: first, the uniqueness of the Lebanon War and its moral complexity; second, the personal/moral characteristics of the Israeli soldiers who refused to serve in Lebanon; and, third, some thoughts on the credibility of the soldiers' moral justifications for their actions.

The Moral Complexity of the Lebanon War

Since its establishment in 1948, the state of Israel with its 3.5 million Jewish citizens has had a continuous struggle for physical survival as it is surrounded by over 100 million Arab neighbors who have never accepted its right to exist (with the exception of the recent peace treaty with Egypt). The Lebanon War (1982–1985) was the sixth war this country experienced during its short years of existence. These wars included the War of Independence (1948–1949, with all the Arab countries), the Sinai campaign (1956, Egypt), the Six Day War (1967, Egypt, Syria and Jordan), the War of Attrition (1967–1970, with Egypt) and the Yom Kippur War (1973, with Egypt and Syria).

Unlike the above 'no-choice wars' (with the exception of the Sinai campaign), the Lebanon War was initiated by Israel (a fact that does not negate the possibility of its being a just war, but obviously demands more clarification and solid argumentation for its moral position).[5]

It is important to note that the war in Lebanon was not planned in a social and moral vacuum. In addition to the "conventional" wars cited above, Israel knew continuous attacks of terrorists from the very first day of its existence. These attacks were escalated during the seventies, mainly by the PLO (Palestinian Liberation Organization) which was forcefully expelled from Jordan where it disrupted civilian life and threatened government stability. When denied permanent settlement and independent action by Syria, the PLO infiltrated into the state of Lebanon which has a long border along the northern region of Israel named Galilee. There, from 1965 to 1982, the PLO's terrorists (and other competing Arab terrorist groups) indiscriminately killed 689 and wounded 3799 Israelis in various attacks within the country. By 1982, 326 Israelis had been killed and 768 were wounded within and outside Israel: for example, the hijacking of the El Al airliner to Algiers (in 1968); the machine-gunning of airline passengers at Ben Gurion Airport (May 30, 1972), where twenty-six were killed and eighty wounded, and in Rome (Dec. 17, 1973), where thirty-one were killed and thirty wounded; and the February 1970 mid-air explosion of a Swiss Air jetliner, which killed forty-seven passengers on its way to Israel. One of the bloodiest atrocities occurred in the town of Maalot in Galilee, where twenty-four elementary school children were murdered and sixty-two others wounded after being held hostage in their classrooms for more than twelve hours. These activities reached their peak on March 11, 1978, when terrorists landed on Israel's coast, hijacked two public buses near Tel Aviv, then commandeered them along the main highway, shooting and throwing grenades from the bus windows, killing thirty-three civilians and wounding eighty-two. A week after this attack, the IDF (Israeli Defense Forces) launched into Lebanon in order to destroy the PLO bases from which the terrorists came. This limited operation, named after a small river that marked the boundary of the territory of action, the Litani, did not bring an end to the terror. The infiltration into Israel and the intentional attacks on civilians continued (combined with frequent shelling with Russian Katyusha missiles), from the Lebanon border to Galilee. Israeli air strikes and commando raids were unable to stem the growth of the PLO around Israel's northern border.

Throughout the years of Israeli counter attacks, the Israeli Defense Force (IDF) was committed to the concept of "Purity of Arms," which demanded careful and just use of military power and emphasis on strict discrimination between fighting soldiers and innocent civilians even in extreme and desperate situations. In one case, during the 1978 Litani operation, when one officer failed to follow this line of conduct he was severely punished. In spite of the difficulties in fighting terrorists who find refuge within the civilian population, the IDF commanders and soldiers were repeatedly instructed to keep the rule of "Purity of Arms."

Following the attempted assassination of Israel's ambassador to Great Britain, in June 1982, the IDF was instructed by the government to destroy the PLO infrastructure in Lebanon in an estimated thirty-six to seventy-eight hour operation. Due to poor planning and an incorrect political assessment of the situation,[6] the operation lasted much longer. The IDF suffered heavy casualties (exceeding the number of terrorist casualties). The original "Peace for the Galilee" campaign turned into a three year occupation of Lebanon and a war with the guerillas in the area.

Most of the soldiers who were morally troubled by the prolongation of the war chose to express their objections as civilians upon their return from reserve service in Lebanon. They argued that the solution of their moral dilemmas should not division their loyalty to the army, which is a central institution *within* the Israeli society and whose impact on the Israeli society goes far beyond its military functions.[7] They tried to solve their moral dilemmas as critics within the army, and to prevent wrongdoing in the battlefield in order to preserve their moral principles there. Upon their return from the service, they protested in front of the government offices. Of course, one may argue that some of them simply did not have the courage to step *outside* the system and perform an action of disobedience within the Israeli society. Though the war was morally controversial, disobedience within the IDF, as long as an illegal command was not given to the soldier, was publicly condemned. Since its establishment in 1948, Israel has known only few cases of conscientious objection;[8] and when they occurred, they did not attract the public's attention since the individuals were regarded as extremists. Nevertheless, in September 1983, when my study started, there were already eighty-six instances of soldiers who refused to serve in Lebanon, claiming that this service would contradict their moral convictions. Overall, during the three years of war, 143 cases were reported.

These 143 known cases might be viewed by an outside observer as an insignificant number. However, given the small size of the state of Israel, the proportion is quantitatively impressive, and, moreover, it marks a dramatic qualitative change in the traditional dedication and commitment of the Israeli soldier/civilian to the IDF and the concept of national security. The Israeli public was faced with a case of moral disobedience in its most dramatic form, on July 27, 1982, when an IDF spokesman announced that Colonel Elli Geva, a brilliant career officer who was among the strong advocates of the war against the PLO, had asked to be released from his position as commander and to serve as a simple soldier. Geva, who commanded a tank brigade that was the spearhead of the fighting up the Beirut/Damascus Road, objected to a planned military move toward conquering Beirut, the capital city of Lebanon,—in order to expell the terrorists who were hidden there. Geva claimed that as a commander he could neither accept responsibility for the civilian casualties likely to be caused nor face the prospect of justifying the action to the families of those in his unit who would be killed. Geva's request caused deep confusion among middle and senior ranking IDF officers, and it became a target of condemnation by many soldiers in his brigade as well as the general public. Geva was dismissed from the army in the midst of the fighting. The planned operation to enter Beirut was abandoned as well.

There was no known case of refusal before Geva's action. Obviously, his action marked a new mode of protest for the simple soldier, who is less free in his contacts with the authorities than the high ranking officer. The fact that a highly respected and patriotic career officer had to take such an extreme action within the IDF in order to preserve his moral integrity seemed to serve as a catalyst for soldiers who searched for an individualistic mode of protest.[9] One refuser in the sample put it in this way: "Before Geva, there was no model of refusal that a soldier could act according to. Certainly this is a very radical action and in my opinion it has to be given in a suitable situation. I could never before think of refusals in my mind, certainly not before the war has . . . broken out."

Who, then, were the Israeli soldiers who chose to act in this manner?

The Moral Personality of the Refusers

Out of the eighty-six reserve soldiers who refused to serve in Lebanon and were imprisoned within the first year of the war, thirty-six were randomly selected for interviewing. Their ages ranged between twenty-three and forty-six years (mean thirty-one; mode twenty-eight), and they came from three main cities in Israel and five kibbutzim. Sixteen were married (eleven with children), five were divorced (four with children), and fifteen were single. Twenty-three had academic degrees including four Ph.D.'s, and three were doctoral candidates (mean 14.9 years of study). This group included seven officers up to the rank of captain. Twenty-two (61 percent) had military experience in war prior to this conflict. Twenty-six (72 percent) refused after serving in Lebanon. Thirty subjects (83 percent) were the only refusers in their unit. Twenty-four (68 percent) served in the occupied territories prior to the Lebanon experience. Twenty-eight (78 percent) did not make any attempt to convince others. Thirty subjects (83 percent) asked to return to their unit upon their release from prison. In terms of political orientation, three defined themselves as Communists, eighteen as Zionist leftists, and fifteen as close to the orientation of the Labor Party.

Each refuser was interviewed (two to four hours) individually in his home by the author upon his release from prison. Each was asked to justify his decision, to relate his personal military experience, and to undergo Kohlberg's psychological test of moral development.[10] It was hypothesized that the soldiers' claim of moral superiority would be manifested in their ability to adhere to principled moral thinking as well as consistency in reasoning between their hypothetical moral competence and justification of their concrete actions.

The demographic data suggest that the Israeli conscientious objector during the war in Lebanon was actually a *selective* conscientious objector. He can be portrayed as a college graduate, and when over 30, with family and children, who fought in former wars, including the Lebanon War. The findings indicate that 44 percent of the subjects were originally postconventional moral thinkers, and that 36 percent manifested postconventional thinking when justifying their concrete action. While it cannot be argued that all the subjects were acting out of principled moral thinking, the percentage of such people in the present study is higher than expected (although precise data on the level of postconventional moral reasoning among comparable groups of Israeli males is not readily available). The highly significant correlation between the soldiers' hypothetical and actual moral reasoning ($r = .89$ p $<.001$) suggests an impressive mode of moral consistency.

The refusers' major argument revolved around the idea that though it is *usually* wrong to disobey in the Israeli Defense Forces as long as the command is legal, it was justified in the specific circumstances of the Lebanon War which deviated from their existing concepts regarding the objectives of a just war and the way it should be handled. The following is an example given by a soldier who could have obtained a release from the army due to kidney disease:

Israel has enormous problems of survival, and we have more wars waiting for us. We cannot allow ourselves to make wars in vain. A condition of going to war is that our lives are severely threatened. The second requirement is that we have done all we can to remove the threat. Only then I feel that the war is just and that I am obliged to do all I can to take part in it.

A significant number of refusers (69.4 percent) exercised at least Stage 4 moral reasoning, which indicates that they took their action on the basis of the understanding of the illegality of refusal within the IDF. The generality of stage 4 moral argumentation might reflect the soldiers' deep concerns regarding collective security[11] and the ideal belief that the validity of one's moral claims emerged from membership in the unit:

> I am close to forty years old, and I took part in every war since I was eighteen years old . . . [due to my profession] I could easily be transferred to a unit where I could serve in an office and not on the battlefield . . . am not going to do so since I feel it would be an escape to close my eyes and say to myself—I am OK, I got out. This is not right because although I solve *my problem* my friends in the unit do the work. I want to return to my unit upon release from prison since by the fact that I continue to serve and remain part of the unit, I buy myself the right to criticize and the right to shout.

Although the principled subjects were expected to be consistent in their stage of moral reasoning across contexts, it was surprising that conventional thinkers (those refusers who, in line with Kohlberg's theory, are susceptible to situational and personal influences upon their actions) were consistent as well. This finding might be attributed to all the refusers' personal "courage to be alone"[12] and their ability to be active (rather than passive) in the construction of their disobedient action.[13] At this level of inquiry, Kohlberg's theory cannot provide a comprehensive psychological account for those who are "actively" capable of acting morally but cannot achieve the highly moral stage of reasoning. The question of **DO** and **HEAR** remains a psychological challenge.

Credibility and the Moral Personality

Credibility, as defined by Feeney,[14] refers to the weight given to admissible testimony. This characteristic is a crucial factor in any decision-making regarding a witness' entitlement to belief. It has a special weight in decision-making regarding an individual who refuses to perform his obligations as a citizen in the name of moral superiority, i.e., the conscientious or selective conscientious objector.

Unlike other witnesses, the CO or SCO does not intend to be "objective" or "unbiased" in his testimony. To some extent, he demands that we understand and judge his action in line with his subjective conscience. As noted by Childress:

"Conscience is personal and subjective. It is a person's conscientiousness and reflection on his own acts in relation to his standard of judgments."[15]

If conscience is personal and subjective, there is a possibility that conscientious and selective conscientious objection might be asserted deceptively. Obviously, the evaluation of actions which are based on subjective conscience is not a simple task. It may suggest, as noted by Emler that: "If each individual has a unique and private view of morality, which guides his conduct, what he does will make little sense to others, and he will have considerable difficulty making himself understood. If anyone does develop a private view, he nonetheless has the problem sooner or later of persuading others to accept his view."[16]

Even if conscientious or selective conscientious objection is genuine and objective, its immediate result within the military setting, particularly in time of war, is extra risk and greater likelihood of casualties for those who are left in the unit and obliged to carry the burden of this "conscientious" behavior.[17] Moreover, "If, in obeying his conscience another man is obliged to do what he believes—in good conscience—to be morally wrong, the genuineness of that conflict must give us a pause."[18]

Assuming that those remaining in the unit have a conscience also (whether subjective or objective) the primary question for consideration, quite before any attempt to assess the correctness of the objector's mode of moral solution, is the credibility of his claim for moral superiority. Credibility is thus a crucial dimension in the attempt to evaluate the claims and actions of conscientious or selective conscientious objectors, particularly if we believe that "the principle of respect for persons does not require respect for the insincere conscience."[19]

Psychological Understanding
of Moral Argumentation—Kohlberg's View

While extremely important, the task of assessing credibility is not a simple one, in part, because of the lack of moral consensus. In his book *Concepts of Just War*, Melzer delineates the complexity of this task as the following: "the task of clarifying the concept of 'acting conscientiously' is itself very difficult, let alone the task of judging conscientiousness in particular cases 'questions to which God alone can know [the answer].' "[20]

Among leading psychological theories on morality, Kohlberg's cognitive developmental approach presents a more formalistic objective moral perspective.[21] Kohlberg assumes the existence of universal justice principles which might be exercised by a person who is capable of reasoning rationally. Morality refers to universal principles which regard the human being as an end rather than a means. The focal point in the assessment of the individual's morality is the mode of choice employed in resolving standardized hypothetical dilemmas of conflicting rights. A moral dilemma is one which revolves around moral issues such as life, law, punishment and conscience, property and affiliation, which are the concern of adults within any culture.[22]

By tracing the way in which the individual prescribes and values the socially good and right, i.e., his moral judgments, Kohlberg believes that we are able to penetrate beyond the subject's opinions, attitudes or beliefs to the reasoning or justifications which direct them. There are two presuppositions to this theory: (1) there is a pattern of connection within the individual's system of meaning, that is, a structure or set of relations and transformation of ideas, and (2) that the interviewer/researcher can understand the interviewee in terms of the meaning he finds in the world and be able to define his framework of thinking at a given stage of development (i.e., an underlying thought organization which undergoes qualitatively formal age-related change).

With the increase in the individual's stage of moral development (from the most primitive Stage 1 up to the utopian Stage 6 of self-chosen ethical principles which are not found in real life practice),[23] the ability to understand and adopt prescriptive, universal justice equity principles increases as well. Life becomes a central issue at Stage 5 in that it becomes a universal intrinsic right.

However, a refusal to take part in a war does not imply that the actor has achieved Stage 5 moral understanding. The action of going to war or refusing to go to war is morally meaningless unless it emerges from moral reasoning. Yet, justification, per se, is not enough—some justifications are more morally adequate than others (i.e., those emerged from the principled rational stages: 5 and 6, and which entail more objective judgment of the conflicting situation and obligations than lower stage reasoning). Moreover, the ability to justify conscientious or selective conscientious objection using the most elaborated justice principles does not encompass the whole complexity of the situation for the objector as well as for the one who must assess his actions.

First, it is questionable whether Kohlberg's justice principles indeed cover the span of real life moral considerations. Obviously, they lack elaborated principles of care, personal responsibility, and loyalty which are so crucial in real life conflicts.[24] Second, the more elaborated stage of moral reasoning does not imply that the person would, or would be entitled to, perform the right action at the right moment. Walzer puts it this way: "How can he be certain that he is right? What if the principles for which he spends his courage and stakes his life turn out to be silly, trivial or fanatic?"[25]

In spite of criticism, Kohlberg's test[26] is known to be one of the most valid and common tests of moral development[27] and has dominated the field of moral psychology in the last two decades. Yet it is important to bear in mind that this test (probably like most psychological tests on morality) is biased in favor of highly verbal (and sometimes educated) individuals.

This bias does not contradict our expectations of selective conscientious objectors. More than universal conscientious objectors, they are expected to be verbally articulate in their self-presentation: "Since conscientious objection of the more limited sort involves the reflective consideration of means and ends, it is more likely rather than less likely to be the outcome of an intelligent and reliable moral judgment."[28]

How, then, should we examine the morality of their claims and credibility of their personality?

Acting Conscientiously—The Search for Consistency

There is some degree of consensus among social researchers that the most salient personal characteristic of CO's or SCO's is their ability to manifest "consistency" or "integrity" in their actions.[29]

When deciding to detach himself from the shared moral meaning of the group, the objector often suggests that this action is the only way in which he can be "true" to his moral self, and that "there is no other way" in which his conscience could remain intact. The validation of this deliberate moral choice is not only the responsibility of the objector but also our duty: At some point, indeed, he may have to stand alone and define his personal integrity against his fellow citizens. "But this is hard to do, and we ought not to pretend that it is (morally) easy. Nor ought we make it easy."[30]

The Kohlbergian method of examining the meaning of arguments would guarantee that the task of self-justification would not be easy. Thus, the objector would have to explain what he means by, and how he understands, phrases as "just" or "unjust" war, "moral" or "immoral" commands, etc. (We often hear the argument of ex-Nazi soldiers who claim that they were fighting a "just war.") However, the target of examination should be their justification of the rightness in the liquidation of an inferior nation. In addition to the quest for the meaning of words and concepts, the objector should be confronted with counter-arguments and further examined for his persistence and ability to adhere to a coherent notion of moral action.

Within Kohlberg's theory, moral consistency is traditionally referred to as consistency in the structure, not the content, of the subject's argumentation, i.e., to a correspondence between a stage of moral development and level of justification of real life action (and not between a certain belief and an action): "People's verbal moral values about honesty have nothing to do with how they act. People who cheat express as much or more moral disapproval of cheating as those who do not cheat."[31]

Kohlberg believes that stage consistency is more likely to occur in the case of those individuals who are competent principled thinkers. Theoretically, the higher the stage of moral development, the higher the likelihood that the person would be able to act consistently with his principles since "One cannot follow moral principles (Stages 5 and 6) if one does not understand or believe in them."[32] However, the ability to present objective rational justice argumentation, while it might be theoretically necessary, is not a sufficient measure of the individual's credibility.

The Search for Credibility:
The Israeli Experience with the SCO
During the Lebanon War

The individual's understanding of justice principles does not guarantee that they are honestly held or believed. Particularly when one's own life is at stake, as in a war situation, they might be used as an excuse for not doing one's own duty, a cover for fear or even for revolutionary plans. Goffman, for example, would argue that as a public action, objection is not only problematic for the audience but also for the actor who wants to influence the interpretation of his action and to create a better impression of its concrete appearance and consequences.[33] Though objection is also an act of isolation, it is not performed in a social vacuum but rather within a network of relationships where actions are ranked for their moral nature.[34]

There is reason to believe that the CO's and the SCO's want to know how their action has been interpreted. Within the Israeli context, where Orthodox Jews are allowed (by political agreement) the status of CO's,[35] the phenomenon of Selective Conscientious Objection is not common. The IDF (Israeli Defense Forces) is conceived, as its name implies, as a defense force which intends to operate on the premise of "Purity of Arms."[36] Traditionally, active service in the IDF from age 18--21 and the life-long reserve service of a month a year up to age 55 which follows were viewed as a crucial moral commitment of any Israeli citizen.

Given the fact that many religious Jews serve in the IDF and that Jewish law dominates the army's regulations, the objector's action is most commonly interpreted as secular evasion of service and requires some detailed explanation from the soldier. The decision of a secular or religious soldier to detach himself from performing the civil obligations of serving in the army is also a psychological turning point in the construction of one's own moral identity within this culture.[37] This refuser explains:

> I guess it is easier for the Israeli public to cope with conscientious objectors rather than with selective conscientious objectors not only because the law protects them but because they are consistent—they just do not take part in any war in this country and do not fulfill any military obligation. We, however, always do the job, protecting

them, and we are not supposed to step out and say: just a minute, this war I am not fighting. By doing so, the public do not like people who are unpredictable.

Another soldier puts it this way:

> It is easier for the public not to be in a dilemma. I guess most of the people use the words *democracy* and *law* in order *not* to think and in order to cover the individual's conscience so they would not have to be in a dilemma. On the other side, they all look at us, those who have a dilemma, as *weak* and as a *proof* that we are wrong.

As we can see from the above quotations, the question of credibility is also, to some extent, a concern of the refusers themselves and might hold some interesting connection to the formation of the whole action. Following the Kohlbergian theoretical framework, selective conscientious objection might be asserted from four possible positions:

1. being morally developed and credible,
2. being morally undeveloped and credible,
3. being morally developed and incredible,
4. being morally undeveloped and incredible.

Position 4 is the easiest to dismiss; position 1, the easiest to accept. Positions 2 and 3 are the hardest to assess: position 2 might include those individuals who are not verbally capable of presenting their perceived moral conflict, or the uneducated, who also might be undergoing a sincere moral struggle. Position 3 might be the classic example of a person who would mislead us due to his verbal skills and impressive Goffmanian self-presentation. How, then, should we go about testing these positions? While there are no ready psychological answers and tests in response to this question, we can still have the opportunity to learn from the real life experience of the Israeli commanders when faced with the dilemma of credibility in judging their refusing soldiers. In some way, their method of inquiry followed the path suggested by Walzer: "We want to know: how he reached his decision, how honestly he confronted his obligations, how seriously he weighed the alternative courses of actions and considered their likely consequences for others as well as for himself."[38]

Let us examine the credibility of the Israeli selective conscientious objectors in line with these guidelines.

Reaching the Decision to Disobey: "In order to disobey," said psychologist Erich Fromm, "one must have the courage to be alone."[39] As indicated before,[40] this courage was the main ("nonmoral") personal characteristic of the refusers: most of the Israeli SCO's made their decision in a lonely manner; eighty-three percent were the only soldiers in their unit to do so.

It is important to point out that the decision to refuse might be divided into two phases: the first of which is the process prior to the overt declaration of refusal; the second starts from the declaration up to the adjudication of the claim. This lonely courage is obviously experienced in the two steps of the action. Let us examine the first phase of the decisionmaking process.

The lonely courage to refuse might have been inspired by contextual factors:

1. Not having a unit of their own due to their military role; most striking with the IDF are the combatant medics who would be transferred from one unit to the other according to the army's needs.[41]
2. Being new in the unit (this war was their first reserve service in the unit).
3. Having a poor relationship with the commander or comrades, or dissatisfaction with the military role.
4. Holding an extreme political stand which the rest of the unit did not share.

When treated as an outsider, the decision to refuse was easy:

> Prior to the war, I was already an outsider in my unit. I had many verbal clashes with the other soldiers in terms of ideology and government policy. I knew that at least on the hypothetical level, I was completely detached from the others. But the real problem was the actual detachment—that you are refusing and going to prison. The same bus that took me to the prison, continued with them to Lebanon. I felt very bad that they would feel cold and I would be warm in prison, but the dominant feeling was that I was not part of them anyhow.

The second phase arises after the declaration on intention to refuse. At this point it must be said that many "moral" refusers claimed that they originally did not want to refuse, but rather "not to serve in Lebanon" hoping that the commanders would grant them this permission. This, however, was not the case with the "political" objectors who were looking for the opportunity to manifest their protest. In most of the cases, although the immediate commander had the right and the obligation to sentence the objecting soldier, he chose to have a thorough discussion with the soldier, even if all the unit had to wait for this procedure.

Due to the life-long service in the reserves, Israeli commanders are well acquainted with the soldiers in their unit (a fact that serves as a partial answer to the next section "how honestly he confronted his obligations"). Particularly "good" soldiers (defined in the next section as morally rather than politically motivated) whom the commander did not want to lose, were given much time to present their objection. Here is an example of a "good soldier" from an armored unit who decided to refuse after he was called on to perform reserve service in Lebanon following two months of combat:

The Major knew me very well. He knew that I did not want to go to Lebanon out of moral reasons and that I am willing to pay the price. He was willing to release* me since he knew that I was a dedicated soldier, but the problem was that he had other soldiers as well: How would he know that those who are refusing after me indeed do it out of moral reasons? and this is indeed a very hard question, and I really understood him. So I sent him a letter. He opened it and said, "OK, I will release you." This is what he was thinking about me as an individual. But I knew that he is also a battalion commander and he has hundreds more people under his command, and there is no way to hide it when he is asked where I am ... and when he faced all of the constraints he decided that he could not prefer me over the others ... and that he could not give up in my case though I knew that he wanted to respond to my request very much. There might be a possibility that all the battalion would refuse and he would have to believe that they are sincere and he would pay with his position. Finally, instead of forty days** in prison, he gave me fourteen.

There seem to be two reasons for the spontaneous efforts used by the commanders in attempting to avoid punishing the objectors. First, the commanders conveyed the distinction that should be made between objection on moral grounds and a regular disciplinary offense. Naturally, it gave the soldier an immediate feeling of worth, and an attitude of respect. Second, particularly in the case of the morally (versus politically) motivated refusers, the commanders acknowledged that these were soldiers who were assets to the unit. Why dismiss them?

The commander's caring attitude did not end by listening and discussing the issue with the soldier. When it became clear that the commander would have to sentence the soldier, he made the soldier fully aware of the context in which the action was taken and its potential consequences for himself and the others. The above refuser continues:

Five minutes before the brigade is about to go to Lebanon and everybody is on the bus, the Major told me, "now you stay five minutes alone, without anyone and you make the final decision, and you have to know that after this time, I will have to sentence you." I told him, "I do not need this five minutes; I am not going with you and that's it. I don't need even one second," but he said, "No, you would think another five minutes . . ." and I guess he was right from his point of view, because even though my thoughts were consolidated by this time, this was a very hard process. These five minutes seemed forever. I guess he wanted to be in peace with himself that he did all that he could in order to convince me to go to Lebanon. I will appreciate it for the rest of my life . . . and this is one of the major reasons that I would not want to leave the battalion. After prison, he phoned me at home and asked me how I was feeling.

Given the fact that the IDF is mainly a reserve army, the issue of motivation is crucial. The fact that the large majority of the refusers were previously motivated soldiers seems to affect also the way they perceived their right to refuse. Said one officer, a father of two, who could serve in a professional unit rather than in a combatant unit:

> I am not fulfilling my obligation to the IDF in doing the reserves, in going to war to kill and be killed, only because there is a law, but because I am aware of my responsibility as a citizen. I see the refusal as an equal moral responsibility, and the law should enable me to do so under very definite and specific circumstances.

Apparently, if an Israeli soldier wants to evade the reserve service, he could do it in various ways: by lowering his medical profile; going abroad,[42] or arranging for special release due to business difficulties, etc. Refusal can be just another tactic in this endless list. It is, therefore, important to test the refusal against the soldier's record of motivation and ways of fulfilling obligations. In this sample, one paratrooper was asked by the author: "Why did you not lower your medical profile rather than refusing?" He replied: "I tried, but I did not succeed, so I decided to refuse."

Honesty in Confronting Obligations: The issue of obligation was part of the soldiers' self-respect. They were ready to be judged against it and even developed some measure of moral credibility between themselves according to their record of obligations. This soldier explains what he thinks about his obligations:

> There is one consideration that I do not accept—that others do the work because of my absence. This is not accurate. The burden of the reserves even between the fighting units, let alone between all the units, is not equally shared. I have a friend who did this year 100 days of reserve service, and I (regardless of the fact that I was in prison) was doing 30. And what about those Orthodox, or those who cheat and claim that they are Orthodox and do not serve . . . I am not sure that I chose the easy way when I refused: the sitting in prison, the terrible dilemmas before, and the fact that everybody points a finger toward you and does not want to talk with you is not simple at all.

The major obstacle to fulfilling one's own obligation, particularly during wartime, is fear. However, fear should not be regarded as exclusive to the refusers, but naturally exists among fighting soldiers. The question is: What makes a particular individual incapable of overcoming his fear?

The study of Israeli SCOs suggests that detachment from the unit (whether subjective—a matter of feeling—or objective—due to the military role) is the major contributor to the inability to cope with fear. This was typical of soldiers who came from the lower-middle class and felt isolated from the rest of the elite group. However, the inability to overcome fear might be equally related to the unjust nature of the war as subjectively perceived by this officer: "I am a paratrooper. It is a very scary job—I always fear the jump from the airplane. But here, in the Lebanon War, I could not find the power to overcome my fear. I think I just did not want to." In some cases, the commander would try to find a tactical solution to the fear.

> Before the trial, the commander invited me to talk with him. I told him that though the war is unjust and is a big mistake and that I am not going to Lebanon and finally that I do not want to die. He told me that if the reason is fear then we both can cope with it, and that he would put me in bunker where I would not have to go out and fight. I think there is something in what he said. Come to think about it, I realized that it was indeed the fear that prevented me from going to Lebanon. It was not the fear to die, but the unwillingness to die. I think I do not want to die for Arik Sharon [the Minister of Defense].

Intuitively, the commander tended to judge the soldier's disobedience, even if performed out of fear, against his record of obligations. This attitude is reflected in the degree of the punishment's severity. "Good" soldiers, as well as "morally" motivated soldiers, were not given the maximum punishment (thirty-five days).

It might be speculated also that less severe punishment is one of the ways in which the commanders tried to convey their sympathy with the soldier's arguments. It also, might be regarded as the commanders' protest against the political or military establishment for making them serve as judges in a war that was morally puzzling in their eyes as well, or for calling them to fight a war they cannot morally win.

Yet, when sentencing, the commanders did not "make it easy" for the soldiers, as dictated by Walzer.[43] One medic described it this way:

> The trial was the critical moment for me. I almost gave up. You're given the feeling that you are a traitor and deserter of your country and that there is a war and that you come in the middle and say that you are not going in. It is a very hard feeling, and I am glad that I did not surrender to it. The Lieutenant Colonel who sentenced me gave me twice during the trial an opportunity to withdraw from my decision to refuse. But I was stubborn and, at the end, he said that he was sorry that he had to jail me. He gave me an attitude of understanding. The fact is that he did not use all his authority in sentencing me to thirty-five days and gave me twenty-eight. Maybe he felt that there is something in what I said.

It is not surprising that both the army and the politicians had an interest in keeping the number of refusers low. Paradoxically, it was also the concern of the unit commanders who, in addition to all the misfunctioning of the IDF and their own moral dilemmas with the war, could not allow themselves the "luxury" of having many refusers in the unit. With the mounting number of refusers, IDF officials initiated a regulation which required a refuser to talk with a psychologist before he was eligible to go to trial. One refuser told the author of a commander who instructed him to have the talk with the psychologist in Lebanon: "I refused, telling my commander that there are enough psychologists within the green line." Another regulation was issued in April, 1983, requiring commanders to immediately call up again any soldier sent to military prison for refusing to serve. Fifteen refusers out of 143 were punished more than once. In this sample, out of thirty-six soldiers, three were repeatedly jailed up to ninety-nine days. Given the fact that the domestic economy's inflation rate was 400% and that most of the refusers had children, repeated jailing also had severe economic and emotional consequences.

Following the threat of repeated jailing, some refusers considered a different approach saying, "I do not want to spend [my] life in prison—next time, I will evade service by other means." Others said, "I made my protest; I cannot sit in prison forever, next time I will have to go to Lebanon."

Obviously, the idea of additional imprisonment shaped the refuser's future calculation. Explains one refuser: "The refusal the second time is harder since the conflict is more sharp. OK, you know what prison looks like, you know that you would not like it once again, you also know that you made a statement and made all the impression you wanted. There are some who now are ready to make concessions."

Motives for Actions and Considerations of Consequence: It is important to note that none of the Israeli SCOs refused while fighting during the first months of the war but, rather, when called for a reserve service during the occupation of Lebanon. There seem to be several reasons for this phenomenon:

1. Refusal during war may entail severe punishment. This was manifested in the case of Elli Geva who was dismissed from the army when he refused to command his soldiers on a mission which he perceived as immoral.
2. The belief that the war would be short.
3. The gradual realization that the war had deteriorated, and that they were involved in a no-win situation in the original fight against terrorists who found refuge among innocent civilians.
4. The realization that the service in Lebanon was a reserve service, which meant that there were various ways in which it could be evaded or objected.

When attempting to assess the motivation of the Israeli SCOs, Cohen's distinction between moral and politically motivated acts of disobedience seems to be helpful. Distinguishing motives is not simple. He explains:

Human motivation is rarely simple. Behind the act of the most honest and scrupulous civil disobedient are likely to lie numbers of intertwined motivating principles: about some, the disobedient himself may be unconscious or unclear. Determining the "real" motivation in a particular case is therefore a messy and uncertain business. But, often one can arrive at some fair judgment in this matter usually with the candid help of the protester himself. Both the appraisal of his character and the understanding of situations in which disobedient protest is employed will be aided by a classification of the kinds of motivation that are commonly operative in such situations. Moral motivation and political motivation are the two major categories. Politics and morals cannot be separated, but they can be distinguished.[44]

The differences are summed up in the following table.

Motivation for disobedience
(constructed from Cohen)[45]

POLITICAL	MORAL
1. Aims at a global change or elimination of injustice by public statement.	1. Less ambitious aims than political—It is mainly the inability to comply in good conscience.
2. Addresses the members of the community at large.	2. Limited in object—It is a response to a direct conflict between the person and the law of the state.
3. Intends to influence the conduct of the people in the community. Its effectiveness must be judged by the extent to which the protest speeds or otherwise advances the envisaged change.	3. More specific in intent—The basic consideration is not the results to which the disobedience leads but the principles.
4. The public performance is crucial.	4. May or may not be performed in public.
5. Essentially a tactic. Whether it be a good tactic depends on what is likely to ensue, in a given case, from its practice: whether the long range goals of its practitioner are advanced.	5. Concrete outcome of deep ethical convictions—Its tactical functions are secondary at best; its practitioners may reply to the objection that it will not prove a wise move simply by saying that it is unfortunate but beyond their control.
6. Hopes to produce change through pressure (public embarrassment), confrontation (mainly by massive demonstrations) or resistance (advising others to do the same).	6. May or may not have some tendency to produce desired political change.

Cohen further explains that morally motivated disobedience may have a political import—import for the whole community—just as politically motivated disobedience may have moral import. "But in being differently conceived and differently aimed, the two kinds of acts may reasonably be distinguished from one another."[46]

Without reading Cohen's book, the Israeli commanders intuitively tried to distinguish between moral and political objectors when attempting to assess the credibility of their refusing soldiers. Political objectors (who might hold good moral intentions) were not treated favorably due perhaps to the great emphasis on the non-political nature of the IDF. As noted by the Israeli law professor, Ruth Gabison,[47] the political objector carries the message that one who does not refuse is committing an immoral action and that their's is the way all the people in the community should follow. However, this political appeal is dangerous since it may be seen as a threat to the entire system of the law, and for this reason, the claims of political objectors should not be respected.

Most of the political objectors, in the sample of this study, claimed that "as soon as the war started, I knew right away that it is not my war." Prior to their decision to refuse, they tended to visit the prison, talk with ex-prisoners about their experiences, etc. The moral objectors usually refrained from such actions. They also did not want their names published, while this was important to the political objectors.

However, due to the fact that the selective conscientious objector was a new qualitative phenomenon, the Israeli public tended to address the refusers as mainly "politically" motivated, even if they were morally motivated. Consequently, both types of refusers suffered in their civil life from their action. Due to the real threat to the country and the blurred distinction between the military and civil life, a secular refusal to serve in the IDF is viewed as a deviant action, and that stigma may reach into the civil life as well. Thus, for example, in the Israeli society, civilian hiring decisions are often based on the applicant's military record. Therefore, commanders in most cases—at least in cases involving morally motivated soldiers—attempted to avoid sentencing and the consequent imposition of stigma. Explained one refuser:

The commander offered me a compromise, which personally, it really humiliated me—that I will come with the unit to Lebanon so I will not have a stigma of refusal, assuming that I would not be called next times—a kind of agreement between me and the Major. This is very easy because it solves the problem. Now I am going with a stigma, and when I come to my battalion, I come as a refuser with a stigma, but when I go to Lebanon, it is forgotten both in the army and in the workplace, and this procedure really solves a small problem to me and a big problem for the rest of the people. But, I am not ready for this compromise. The problem cannot be swept under the carpet. Things stand and fall on this issue.

At the other extreme, there were commanders who did not seek an easy release for their morally motivated soldiers, but approached all of them as having political import; and consequently, they tried to find more severe punishments. In one rare case, a dedicated soldier, who in a fighting unit decided to refuse, not only received the full term of imprisonment but when later chosen in his civil life to be an Israeli representative to the U.S. Jewish community, (a job which would also help him in his desperate financial situation), was hindered by his commander who objected to civil authorities, and the soldier did not get the job.

The stigma was not only an obstacle between the refuser and the society but also between the refusers themselves. One of them explained: "I thought that those who refuse and belong to Yesh Gvul [the refusers' protest movement] are a bunch of communists, anti-Zionists, and stubborn people, and I had some fear in being included among them if I refuse. It was quite a dilemma."

Obviously, the politically motivated refusers were less concerned about the stigma than the morally motivated soldiers. Both, however, considered the action as a painful one (although some politically motivated soldiers said they "enjoyed" it) and both awaited some immediate consequences of their action—either to themselves or the community or both. However, given the fact that when they came out of prison, there was still war and another draft awaited them sooner or later, their dilemma was not resolved. Concluded one refuser: "I was surprised to realize when I came out of prison that most of the people did not care what is going on in the country around them. I was shocked. I thought that I would change the world, but I did not."

Conclusion

The Israeli sample portrays a heterogeneous group of selective conscientious objectors: some experienced loneliness in their decisionmaking process; some could not overcome their fear of war; some were inspired by political groups; and others claimed to be morally motivated.

The military can help many avoid some of the dilemmas the soldiers faced. Attention should be given to the soldier who is not attached to his unit. The soldier who fears should be helped in order to regain confidence in the army as well as in himself. The political objector can more easily be punished—at least, he awaits the punishment which gives some effect to his action.

The claim of the moral objector should be assessed against his previous record of fulfilling obligations. Yet, moral argumentation should not be accepted as credible, per se, and should be challenged. An effort should be made to try and work out a solution within the unit. If morality is important to the individual, he should also try and implement his beliefs within the system.

Finally, it is worth noting that mild punishment might be helpful in detecting the individual's credibility. In the Israeli army, punishment might be regarded as mild if it consisted of up to one month in prison, lost pay and allowances for that period, and some form of social hostility. Explained one refuser: "I am glad that the punishment was as mild as it was. First, it showed me the moral strength of the IDF who was not scared of a wave of refusers. Second, it makes me act upon my moral principles. I guess that if the punishment was severe, I would do all what I can to cheat the army and avoid service and not to be punished." There is another benefit to a mild punishment, as noted by this soldier:

> I think that it is quite dangerous to go to prison, and I wonder if all the refusers thought about it ahead of time. You are going to sit among military lawbreakers and this is a defined company. Throughout my time as an officer in the artillery, there were many of my soldiers whom I tried to help, etc., and now I was sitting with them since I was also fighting with the IDF, a fight which I chose to do, and they also had a fight with the IDF, and suddenly I found myself supporting any deserter, etc. I am afraid to think how we all would support these people if the stay in prison would be long.

At least within the Israeli reality of war, selective conscientious objectors should be given more credibility than the Unconditional Objectors who often take advantage of the social system, rather than pointing out its weak points that they are ready to correct.

In this spirit, we can adopt the idea of Albert Camus, who argued that the one who says "No" is also the one who says "Yes": he is the one who affirms the values on the other side of the line. We need to know and make sure that the moral objector is not only the one who refuses to do the immoral, but, is clear and dedicated in doing the moral. This would be an important factor in the assessment of credibility.

Notes

1. J. Loevinger, *Ego Development: Conceptions and Theories,* (San Francisco: Josey-Bass, 1976), p. 277.

2. R. Hogan, J.A. Johnson, N.P. Emler, "A Socioanalytic Theory of Moral Development," in *The Social World of the Child* W. Damon, ed. (San Francisco: Josey-Bass, 1977), p. 14.

3. D.J. Bem, *Beliefs, Attitudes and Human Affairs* (Belmont, CA: Brooks/Cole, 1970).

4. L. Kohlberg, "Moral Stages and Moralization," in *Moral Development and Behavior: Theory, Research and Social Issues,* T. Lickona, ed. (N.Y.: Holt, Rinehart, and Winston, 1976); L. Kohlberg, *The Psychology of Moral Development* (San Francisco: Harper & Row, 1984).

5. M. Walzer, *Just and Unjust Wars, a moral argument with historical illustrations,* (New York: Basic Books, 1977).

6. See for more details Z. Shiff and E. Yaari, *Israel's Lebanon War,* Trans. and ed. Ina Friedman (New York: Simon and Schuster, 1984); S. Shiffer, *Snow Ball—the story behind the Lebanon War* (Arabic), (1985).

7. R. Gal, "Commitment and Obedience in the Military—An Israeli Case Study," *Armed Forces & Society,* 11, 4 (Summer 1985) 553–64.

8. M. Blatt, U. Davis, P. Kleinbaum, *Dissent and Ideology in Israel—Resistance to the Draft (1948–1973)* (London: Ithaca Press, 1975).

9. R. Linn, "Conscientious Objection in Israel During the War in Lebanon," *Armed Forces & Society,* 12, 4 (Summer 1986) 489–511.

10. A. Colby, L. Kohlberg, J. Gibbs, et al., *The Measurement of Moral Judgement: Standard Issue Scoring Manual* (New York: Cambridge University Press, 1983).

11. N. Emler, "Morality and Politics: The Ideological Dimension in the Theory of Moral Development," *Morality in the Making—Thoughts, Action and the Social Context* H. Weinrich-Haste, D. Locke, eds (New York: Wiley, 1983).

12. E. Fromm, *On Disobedience—and other essays* (New York: Seabury Press, 1982), p. 21.

13. R. Linn, "Moral Disobedience During the Lebanon War—What Can the Cognitive Developmental Approach Learn From the Experience of the Israeli Soldiers?" *Social Cognition,* 5 (1988) 383–402.

14. T.J. Feeney, "Expert Psychological Testimony on Credibility Issues," *Military Law Review,* (1987), 115–177 at p. 121

15. J.F. Childress, "Appeals to Conscience," *Ethics* (1979), 89, 4, 315–335 at p. 318.

16. H. Emler, "Moral Character," in H. Weinrich, L. Haste, D. Locke, eds., *Morality in the Making: Thoughts, Action and Social Context,* (1983), pp. 187–212 at p. 207.

17. R. Linn, C. Gilligan, "One Action Two Moral Orientations: The Tension Between Justice and Care Voices Among Selective Conscientious Objectors," *New Ideas in Psychology,* (in press).

18. C. Cohen, *Civil Disobedience—Conscience, Tactics and The Law* (New York, London: University Press, 1971).

19. J.F. Childress, *Moral Responsibility in Conflicts: Essays on Nonviolence, War and Conscience* (Baton Rouge: Louisiana State University Press, 1982), p. 215.

20. Y. Melzer, *Concepts of Just War* (Leyden, Holland: Sijthoff, 1975), p. 174.

21. L. Kohlberg, "Moral Stages and Moralization"; L. Kohlberg, *The Psychology of Moral Development.*

22. A. Colby, L. Kohlberg, J. Gibbs, et al. *The Measurement of Moral Judgement: Standard Issue Scoring Manual* (New York: Cambridge University Press, 1983).

23. J. Gibbs, K.F. Widaman, A. Colby, "Construction and validation of a simplified group administerable equivalent to the moral judgment interview," *Child Development* (1982), 53, 895.

24. R. Linn, C. Gilligan, "One Action Two Moral Orientations."

25. M. Walzer, *Obligations, Essays on Disobedience, War and Citizenship* (Cambridge, Mass.: Harvard University Press, 1970), p. 130.

26. A. Colby, L. Kohlberg, J. Gibbs, et al., *The Measurement of Moral Judgement.*

27. J. Gibbs, "Kohlberg's Stages of Moral Development: A Constructive Critique," *Harvard Education Review* (1978) 13, 33.

28. C. Cohen, "Conscientious Objection,"*Ethics* (1968) 58, 269–279.

29. C. Cohen, *Civil Disobedience—Conscience, Tactics and The Law.*

30. M. Walzer, *Obligations, Essays on Disobedience, War and Citizenship,* p. 130.

31. L. Kohlberg, "Education for Justice: A Modern Statement of the Platonic View," in *Moral Education: Five Lectures,,* N. F. Sizer, ed. (Cambridge, Mass: Harvard University Press, 1970), p. 64.

32. L. Kohlberg, "Moral Stages and Moralization," p. 32; L. Kohlberg, *The Psychology of Moral Development.*

33. E. Goffman, *The Presentation of Self in Every Day Life* (Garden City, N.Y.: Doubleday, 1959).

34. R. Brown and R.J. Herrenstein, *Psychology* (Boston: Little, Brown, 1975).

35. M. Blatt, U. Davis, P. Kleinbaum, *Dissent and Ideology in Israel—Resistance to the Draft (1948–1973).*

36. R. Gal, "Commitment and Obedience in the Military—An Israeli Case Study"; R. Linn, *"Conscientious Objection in Israel During the War in Lebanon."*

37. R. Linn, C. Gilligan, "One Action Two Moral Orientations."

38. M. Walzer, *Just and Unjust Wars.*

39. E. Fromm, *On Disobedience—and other essays.*

40. R. Linn, C. Gilligan, "One Action Two Moral Orientations;" Linn, "Moral Disobedience During the Lebanon War."

41. R. Linn, "The Power to Act Morally—Refusers and Peace Activists Discuss Their Moral Integrity," in preparation.

42. Yediot Acharonot (Israel), January 10, 1985.

43. M. Walzer, *Obligations: Essays on Disobedience, War and Citizenship.*

44. C. Cohen, *Civil Disobedience—Conscience, Tactics and The Law,* p. 22.

45. Ibid, pp. 57–58.

46. Ibid, p. 58.

47. R. Gabison, "The crime of the blue-white collar," *Politic,* April 7, 1986, 28–30 (Hebrew).

Notes on Contributors

George Q. Flynn is a Professor of History at Texas Tech University, and has written extensively on the role of religion in American politics and on the draft. His books include *Lewis B. Hershey, Mr. Selective Service* (1985) and *The Mess in Washington: Manpower Mobilization in World War II* (1979).

Kent Greenawalt is the Cardozzo Professor of Jurisprudence at Columbia University. His books include *Conflicts of Law and Morality* (1987) and *Religious Convictions and Political Choice* (1988). His articles on religious convictions and the law include "Conscientious Objection and the Liberal State" in *Religion and the State* (1984).

J. Bryan Hehir is a priest, Secretary of the Department of Social Development and World Peace of the United States Catholic Conference and Research Professor of Ethics and International Politics at Georgetown University's School of Foreign Service. His articles include "The Relationship of an Ethic of War and a Theology of Peace: Preliminary Ideas," *The Annual of the Society of Christian Ethics* (1984); "The Use of Force and the International System Today," *The Moral Dimensions of International Conflict* (1983); "The Just-War Ethic and Catholic Theology: Dynamics of Change and Continuity," *War or Peace: The Search for New Answers* (1980); "Church and State: Basic Concepts for an Analysis," *Origins* 8 (1978); "International Affairs and Ethics," *Chicago Studies*, 11 (1972); "Nonviolence, Peace and Just-War," *Worldview*, 12 (1969).

James L. Lacy is a Senior Policy Analyst for the Rand Corporation, Washington, D.C. where he works primarily on national security issues. Between 1977 and 1981 he served in the Offices of the Secretary of Defense and Assistant Secretary of Defense for Manpower, Reserve Affairs and Logistics. His publications include "Military Manpower: The American Experience and the Enduring Debate" and "Obligatory Service: The Fundamental and Secondary Choices" in *Toward a Consensus on Military Service* (1982); "The Case for Conscription" in *Military Service in the United States* (1982); *Naval Reserve Forces: The Historical Experience with Involuntary Recalls* (1986); "Whither the All-Volunteer Force," *Yale Law and Policy Review* (Fall 1986).

John P. Langan is a priest, Rose Kennedy Professor of Christian Ethics, Kennedy Institute of Ethics and Department of Philosophy, Georgetown University, and acting Director and Senior Research Fellow, Woodstock Theological Center. He has served as a consultant to the U.S. Navy Chief of Chaplains. His works on moral reasoning and public policy include "Politics—Good, Bad, or Indifferent? A Philosophical Assessment" in *Between God and Caesar* (1985); "Values, Rules, and Decision," in *Personal Values in Public Policy* (1979); "Just War Theory and Decision Making in a Democracy," *Naval War College Review* (July–August, 1985); and "The Elements of Just War Theory in St. Augustine," *Journal of Religious Ethics*, 12 (1984).

Ruth Linn is an Assistant Lecturer at the University of Haifa (Israel) School of Education. Her publications in English include "Conscientious Objection in Israel During the War in Lebanon," *Armed Forces and Society*, 12 (Summer, 1986) and "Moral Disobedience—What Can Cognitive Development Theory Learn from the Experience of the Israeli Reserve Soldiers Who Refused to Serve in Lebanon?" *Social Cognition* 5 (1988). She served in the Israeli Defense Forces 1968–1970.

Michael F. Noone, Jr., is an Associate Professor of Law at The Catholic University of America. He retired as a Colonel after twenty years' service in the U.S. Air Force as a judge advocate. His publications include "Military Social Science Research in Law" (forthcoming, *Armed Forces and Society*); "Rendering Unto Caesar: Legal Responses to Religious Nonconformity in the Armed Forces," *St. Mary's Law Journal*, 18 (1987).

Edward F. Sherman is the Angus G. Wynne Professor of Law at the University of Texas. He served on active duty in the Army between 1965 and 1967 and is a Lieutenant Colonel. His numerous works include "Judicial Review of Military Determinations and the Exhaustion of Remedies Requirement," *Virginia Law Review*, 55 (1969); "Military Courts and Servicemen's First Amendment Right," *Hastings Law Journal*, 22 (1971); "Legal Inadequacies and Doctrinal Restraints in Controlling the Military," *Indiana Law Journal*, 49 (1974) and *The Military in American Society: Cases and Materials* (1979) (co-author).

Walter F. Sullivan, priest and bishop, has served in the diocese of Richmond, Virginia, since his ordination in 1953. The diocese includes major Army, Navy and Air Force installations. He is on the boards of the Churches' Center for Theology and Public Policy and Pax Christi, U.S.A.

William J. Wagner is an Assistant Professor of Law at The Catholic University of America. He is completing work on his Doctorate in Theology and is co-editor of *A Symposium on the Religious Foundations of Civil Rights Law* (forthcoming).

Gordon C. Zahn is National Director of the Center on Conscience and War and Professor Emeritus of Sociology at the University of Massachusetts, Boston. Active in matters relating to morality and nonviolence since World War II, his books include *In Solitary Witness: The Life and Death of Franz Jaegerstaetter* (rev. ed., 1986); *Another Part of the War: The Camp Simon Story* (1979); *The R.A.F. Chaplaincy: A Role in Tension* (1969); *War, Conscience and Dissent* (1967); and *German Catholics and Hitler's Wars* (1962). He edited and wrote the introduction to Thomas Merton's *The Nonviolent Alternative* (1980).

Index

Abortion, 72

Address to the United Nations (Paul VI), 68

Afghanistan, 47

Air Force, 14

Air Force Reserve, 125

All–Volunteer Force, 47–48, 74, 108, 113

Alternative service, 9, 11, 15, 17, 21, 35, 40, 48(n2), 54–55(n60), 58, 84,103,107–108, 111–115
  defined, 108
  during Korean war, 41–42
  during Vietnam War, 46, 54(n58)
  during World War II, 37, 38–39, 51(n33), 57, 58–60, 112, 113–114

American Friends Reconstruction Units, 112

American Friends Service Committee, 41, 114

American Legion, 41

American Revolution, 1

Amish, 102

Amnesty, 50(n20)

Amnesty Program (1974), 120

Anti-war movement, 43, 45

Appeals, 36–37, 38, 40, 49(n50)

Aquinas, Saint Thomas, 53(n51), 64–65, 78(nn 6,7), 96, 99

Arab-Israeli conflict, 131–149

Arms race, 69

Armstrong, Paul G., 35

Augustine, Saint, 53(n51), 64, 65, 77(n4), 77–78(n5)

Azeglio, Taparelli d', 65

Bainton, Roland H., 63

Baptists, 51(n33)

"Basis in fact" test, 120–122

Basker, 112

Berrigan, Phillip, 43–44

Bill of Rights, 2, 28–29

Blacks, 50(n23), 112

Blameworthiness. *See* Moral blameworthiness

Brewster, Kingman, 45

Camus, Albert, 149

Carter, Jimmy, 47, 74

Catholic Church, 43, 50(n23), 51(n33), 63–79, 81–87
  bishops, 25–34, 44, 57, 63, 71–79, 86, 91
  doctrine, 63–71, 82, 91–93, 98
  See also "Just war" concept

CCC. *See* Civilian Conservation Corps

Center on Conscience and War, 57, 85

Central Committee for Conscientious Objectors, 119

Challenge of Peace, The: God's Promise and Our Response, 25, 30, 63, 71, 72, 75, 76, 91–92. *See also* Catholic Church, bishops

Childress, James F., 76, 135–136

Christadelphians, 49(n16)

Christian Attitudes Toward War and Peace (Bainton), 63

Church. *See* Jewish law; "Peace churches"; Religious beliefs; *entries for individual denominations*

Church affiliation, 35–38, 47, 57, 58. *See also* Religious beliefs

Church of God, 49(n16)

Church of the Brethren, 35, 49(n16), 51(n33). *See also* "Peace churches"

Church of the Four Leaf Clover, 51(n33)

Church-state separation, 100

Civil disobedience, 26, 28, 101, 103

Civilian Conservation Corps (CCC), 38, 112

Civilian deaths, 93–94, 98

Civilian Public Service (CPS) program, 57, 58–60, 112

Civilian service, 9. *See also* Alternative service

Civil rights, 90–91, 105, 109
Civil Rights movement, 43, 101
Clark, Grenville, 36
Clark, Mark, 45
Clark, Tom, 44
Classification, 17–21, 32–33
Clemency Board, 112
CO. *See* Conscientious objector classification
Cohen, C., 145–147
Combat duty, 89–90
Concepts of Just War (Melzer), 136
Conformism, 14–15, 16, 22(n5), 103
Conscience. *See* Personal conscience
"Conscience crystallization," 85
Conscientious objection
    criteria, 16–21, 33, 118
    defined, 7
    in Israel, 132–135, 139–149
    in-service, 117–127, 132–135, 139–149
    political motivation of, 146(table), 147, 148
    stage of assertion, 19–20, 32, 85
    See also Exemptions; General objectors
Conscientious objector (CO) classification,
    35–55, 109–110, 112–113
Conscription. *See* Draft
Conscription Act of 1917, 35
Consistency, 138–139
Constitution, 2, 109
Contraception, 72
Courts martial, 122–125
CPS. *See* Civilian Public Service program
Credibility, 135–136, 139–148
Curry, Stauffer, 42

*Declaration on Conscientious Objection and
    Selective Conscientious Objection*,
    25, 72, 73–74, 75
Defense. *See* Self-defense
Deferments, 42, 43
Department of Defense directive, 117–118
Dewey, John, 130
Dignitatis Humanae, 73
Disability concept, 15
Disarmament, 69–70, 79(n30)
Distributive justice, 30–31, 32. *See also* Al-
    ternative service; Fairness
Douglass, James, 66, 68
Draft, 2
    fairness and, 15, 21

government power to, 31
in Korean war, 41
peacetime, 40, 42, 74–75, 85, 108
registration, 39, 40, 47, 48, 74–75
resistance to, 43, 45
during Vietnam War, 43, 45–47, 112, 114
during WWI, 111
during WWII, 39, 112
See also Selective Service System
Draft Act of 1951, 41
Dykstra, Clarence, 37

Egypt, 131
Eisenhower, Dwight D., 42
Emler, H., 136
Episcopal Church, 44
"Equivalency of sacrifice" concept, 38
Exemptions, 10–11, 13–14
    criteria for, 16–21, 33, 118
    justifiability of, 25–34
    scope of, 19, 21
    self-selecting, 21–22
    See also Conscientious objection

Fairness, 15–16, 21, 77
Fear, 139, 144
Federal Republic of Germany, 55(n63)
Feeney, T. J., 135
Finn, James, 76
Fitzsimmons Army Hospital, 51(n33)
Flynn, George Q., 58, 59, 61
Ford, Gerald R., 112, 120
France, 55(n63)
French, Paul Comly, 36, 37
Fromm, Erich, 140

Gabison, Ruth, 147
Gandhi, Mohandas, 26
Gaudium et Spes, 66, 67, 68, 69, 70, 71, 73,
    91
General objectors, 11, 15, 20, 21, 30–31, 36.
    See also Conscientious objection;
    Pacifism
Geva, Elli, 133, 145
Gillette v. United States, 3, 22(n3), 29,
    53(n48)
Globalism. *See* International good
Goffman, E., 139
"Good soldiers," 141, 144

Government Authority, 31, 99–100, 101, 102, 103, 104–105
Great Britain, 55(n63)
Greenawalt, Kent, 25–26, 27–33
Grenada intervention, 14, 101
Grotius, Hugo, 53(n51), 65

Hammond v. Lenfest, 120–121
Harlan, John Marshall, 22(n3), 109
Harrison, Benjamin, 1
Hebert, F. Edward, 45
Hershey, Lewis B., 36, 37–38, 40, 41, 42, 44, 46, 49(n15), 52(n37), 53(n50) 58, 59–60
Hijackings, 131
Holy See and Disarmament at the U.N., The, 68, 69
Humanae Vitae, 72
Human Life in Our Day, 72–73, 74, 75

I-A-O classification, 36, 37
Identification, 16–21, 43, 113, 118, 120–121, 136. *See also* Classification
IDF. *See* Israeli Defense Forces
Imprisonment, 39, 42, 49(n20), 145, 149. *See also* Punishment
Individual conscience. *See* Personal conscience
Integrity. *See* Consistency
International good, 31, 92
International law, 29–30
I-O, 36, 37, 42, 46
Israel, 129, 131–135, 139–149
Israeli Defense Forces (IDF), 132, 133, 134, 135, 139–149
I-W classification, 41, 42, 46. *See also* Alternative service

James, William, 89, 114, 115
JANSSC. *See* Joint Army Navy Selective Service Committee
Jehovah Witnesses, 39, 42, 49(nn 16,20), 52(n37), 55(n60)
Jewish law, 129–130, 139
John Paul II (pope), 70–71, 86
John XXIII (pope), 66–67, 87
Johnson, Lyndon B., 43, 45, 46
Joint Army Navy Selective Service Committee (JANSSC), 36
Jones, Roger, 41

Jones v. Lemond, 124
Jordan, 131
Judicial review, 120–122
Jus ad bellum, 75, 96, 97
Jus in bello, 75, 96
"Just war" concept, 8, 10–11, 19, 20, 27, 30, 45, 53(n51), 57, 63–71, 75, 76, 86, 92–98, 99–101, 102–105, 138

Kennedy, John F., 43
King, Martin Luther, 43
Knaus, Vincent, 35
Knights of Columbus, 81, 82
Kohlberg, Lawrence, 130–131, 134, 135, 136–138
Korean war, 40–42, 51(n32), 101
Kosch, Colonel, 59

Labor camps, 38–39, 59–60, 112, 114
Law of War, 19. *See also* War, legality of
Lebanon war, 131–149
Legality, 8, 18–19, 92
Legal responses, 8–9
Legislation, 103
    Catholic doctrine and, 76–77
    criteria for, 27–28
    influences on, 30
    morality and, 99
Legislators, 26–27, 33
Libyan air strike, 14
Litani operation, 132
Lutherans, 44

McNamara, Robert, 44
Madison, James, 2, 109
Mansfield, John, 111
Marshall, Burke, 45
Marshall Commission, 45, 46, 109
Marshall Report, The, 91, 98–105
Melzer, Y., 136
Mennonites, 35, 49(n16), 51(nn 32,33), 109. *See also* "Peace churches"
Merton, Thomas, 87
Military autonomy, 120–122
Military conformism, 14–15
Military discipline, 31, 32
Military morale, 104–105
Military operations, 14
Military tradition, 1–2

Moliere, 90
Moral blameworthiness, 11–12
Moral culture, 1, 7, 12, 25–26, 30, 31, 33,
    44–45, 76–77, 96–97, 98, 99, 100–103
    105, 129–131, 136–138, 139–140.
    See also Catholic Church, doctrine
"Moral Equivalent of War, A" (James), 114
Morality. *See* Moral culture; Personal
    conscience
Murphy, Frank, 84
Murray, John Courtney, 45, 65
My Lai massacre, 93
My Sunday Missal, 35

National Advisory Commission on Selective
    Service, 45, 91, 98–105
National Conference of Catholic Bishops,
    25–34, 44, 57, 63, 71– 79, 86, 91
National Council of Churches of Christ, 44
National Defense. *See* Self-defense
National Interreligious Service Board for
    Conscientious Objectors (NISBCO), 83,
    84, 85–86
National Service Board of Religious
    Objectors (NSBRO), 37, 40, 41
Natural law, 92
Nazarenes, 109
*Nevertheless: The Varieties of Religious
    Pacifism* (Yoder), 68
New Testament, 130
NISBCO. *See* National Interreligious Service
    Board for Conscientious Objectors
Nixon, Richard, 43, 46, 55(n60)
No First Use policy, 75
Noncombatant duty, 9, 32, 35, 36, 39, 40, 99,
    102–103, 109, 111. *See also*
    Alternative service
Nonreviewability, 120, 121
NSBRO. *See* National Service Board of
    Religious Objectors
Nuclear war, 31
Nuclear weapons, 75, 77
Nuremberg trials, 30, 105

Obligations, 143–145
Oswego County Farmers' Cooperative, 114

Pacem In Terris (John XXIII), 66–67, 68, 69,
    78(n21), 87

Pacific Counseling Service, 122
Pacifism, 1, 2, 12, 18, 20, 43, 66–71, 92,
    109. *See also* General objectors;
    "Peace churches"
Palestine Liberation Organization (PLO),
    131–132
Patriotism, 81–82
Paul VI (pope), 66, 67–68, 70, 72, 79(n30)
Pax Christi, 57, 68, 85
"Peace churches," 2, 29, 35, 36, 38, 39, 41,
    42, 47, 51(n33), 86
"Peace church" model, 58
"Peace for the Galilee" campaign, 132.
    See also Lebanon war
Personal conscience, 28–29, 31, 33, 35, 36,
    37–38, 40, 44, 45, 47, 50(n20), 73, 77,
    95, 99, 102, 104–105, 110, 130–149
"Phu Cat 3, The," 122–123
Pius XII (pope), 65–66, 67, 68, 71, 74,
    78(n13)
PLO. *See* Palestine Liberation Organization
Poland, 98
Political culture. *See* Socio-political culture
Political objection, 146(table), 147, 148
Potter, Ralph B., 68, 76
Public service camps, 38–39, 59–60, 112,
    114
Punishment, 10, 11–16, 17, 28, 39, 144–145,
    148–149. *See also* General objectors
"Purity of Arms" concept, 132, 139

Quakers, 1, 35. *See also* "Peace churches"

Rabbinical Assembly, 44
Ramsey, Paul, 66
Reagan, Ronald, 48
Religious beliefs, 1, 2, 9, 20–21, 22(n3), 33,
    35, 36–38, 40, 42, 44, 45, 47, 50(n20),
    54(nn 55,56), 58, 61, 84, 109–111, 129.
    See also "Peace churches"
Reynolds, Mrs. J. Robert, 45
Roberts, Owen, 50(n20)
Roman Catholic Bishops, 25–34, 44, 57, 63,
    71–79, 86, 91
Roosevelt, Franklin D., 35, 36, 114
ROTC cadets, 125
Rule of law, 27–29, 30, 31. *See also*
    Socio-political culture
Russell, F. H., 77(n4), 77–78(n5)

Second Vatican Council, 66, 67, 69, 70, 73, 74, 75, 91, 92
Selective Service Act (1917), 2, 73, 117
Selective Service System, 35–55, 58, 59, 60–61, 83–86, 111–113, 118
Selective Training and Service Act (1940), 2, 22(n3)
Self-defense, 64–65, 67, 68, 69, 78(n7), 91, 102
Self-justification, 138–149
Sharon, Arik, 144
Society of Friends, 35, 49(n16), 51(n33), 54(n58), 109, 120. *See also* "Peace churches"
Socio-political culture, 1, 14, 30, 31, 47, 85–86, 90–92, 100–102, 147–148
Soviet Union, 40, 47
Spanish Scholastics, 53(n51), 64, 65, 75
Stalin, Joseph, 42
Statement on Registration and Conscription for Military Service, 72, 74–75
Stigma, 147–148. *See also* Socio-political culture
Strauss, 112
Suarez, Francisco, 53(n52), 64, 75
Supreme Court, 14, 20, 22(n3), 44–45, 72, 110–111, 113
Sweden, 55(n63)
Syria, 131

Tarr, Curtis, 46
Tatum, Arlo, 43
Technologies, 31. *See also* Weapons systems
Ten Commandments, 129
Terrorism, 131–132
Torah, 130
Truman, Harry, 40–41, 50(n20)
Turnage, Thomas K., 84

UMT. *See* Universal Military Training
United Church of Christ, 44
United States Catholic Conference (USCC), 83
United States v. Cook, 54–55(n60)
United States v. Lee, 29
United States v. Levy, 54(n55)
United States v. Noyd, 123–124
United States v. Seeger, 2, 22(n3), 33, 44, 45, 110, 117, 123

United States v. Sisson, 53(n48)
Universal Military Training (UMT), 40
USCC. *See* United States Catholic Conference

"Value of Non-Violence, The," 71
Vatican II. *See* Second Vatican Conference
Vietnamization, 46
Vietnam War, 2, 8, 9, 17, 30, 33, 42, 71, 77, 84, 111, 118, 125
   alternative service, 46, 54(n58)
   Catholic bishops' response to, 72, 73, 74, 75
   draft during, 43, 45–47, 112, 114
   in-service COs, 119–120, 122–124
   protest against, 43, 45
Virginia Military Institute (VMI), 81
Vitoria, Francisco de, 64, 75
VMI. *See* Virginia Military Institute
Voltaire, 90

Walters, LeRoy B., 64, 78(n6)
Walzer, M., 140, 144
War, 89
   conduct of, 93–94, 96–98, 102, 104
   crimes, 8
   as foreign policy instrument, 9–10
   "just," 8, 10–11, 19, 20, 27, 30, 45, 53(n51), 57, 63–71, 75, 76, 86, 92–98, 99–101, 102–105, 138
   legality of, 8, 18–19, 92
Washington, George, 1
Weapons systems, 19, 22(n2), 75, 77
Welsh v. United States, 2, 33, 110, 111, 112, 113
Wildavsky, Aaron, 3
Wilson, Raymond, 36, 37, 47
Wisconsin v. Yoder, 29
Work camps, 38–39, 59–60, 112, 114
World Day of Peace Message, 70
World War I, 35, 36, 47, 58, 59
World War II, 36, 49(n15), 51(n32), 55(n63), 93

Yesh Gvul, 148
Yoder, John, 68
Yolton, William, 86

Zahn, Gordon, 84

8420